*"... He who has begun a good work..."*

Philippians 1:6

BY
LINDA GREGORINO

Copyright © 1986

LINDA J'S MINISTRIES
102 N. VINE
COLUMBIANA, OHIO 44408

# Contents

## Part I: Body

Chapter One
    In The Beginning..................................................6
Chapter Two
    Epilepsy? NO, Not Me!......................................13
Chapter Three
    His Hand Of Mercy............................................16
Chapter Four
    Help Comes........................................................21
Chapter Five
    Dream Home......................................................26
Chapter Six
    Heart Surgery....................................................30
Chapter Seven
    Even When Walking Through The Dark Valley...............35

## Part II: Soul

Chapter Eight
    His Ways... Not Mine......................................43
Chapter Nine
    Gil, A Miracle Friend........................................47
Chapter Ten
    The Holy Ghost Is WHAT?...............................51
Chapter Eleven
    Testing and Trial Produce Joy..........................54
Chapter Twelve
    Satan?? The Guy With Horns And A Tail?.......57
Chapter Thirteen
    Presumption......................................................63

## Part III: Spirit

Chapter Fourteen
    Learning Obedience..........................................75
Chapter Fifteen
    HIS Kind Of Love..............................................79
Chapter Sixteen
    It's Not An Easy Road......................................85
Chapter Seventeen
    Back To My Beginning......................................88
Chapter Eighteen
    I Can't Take Anymore!.....................................98
Chapter Nineteen
    A Dress Of Gold..............................................105

Author Linda Gregorino

# Introduction

My prayer is that my story might open you to your own story. For Christ loves you and has begun a good work in you. Look back with me and see Him.

Are you thinking, "Oh, no! Not another testimony book!"? Let's be honest — you are. That's okay. I ask that before you decide not to read this book you consider that it is not just my story but yours.

It's yours for Christ has also begun a good work in you. Did you know that? For a long time I wasn't aware of Christ in my life either. But I've looked back to the road I came and I now see His shepherd's hand has always been there.

He has predestined us to be His children and each and every turn of our lives has been with His knowledge of our needs. We don't always know our needs nor know that He knows. And so His purpose in our age has been to reveal Himself to us by the Holy Spirit.

I look back now and am amazed at my Shepherd's presence. He was with me when I only knew "church," not Christ. He spoke to me when I didn't know He had a voice. His hand of compassion has guided and turned and lifted and held me. And so you . . .

**Mother & Dad**

# Dedication

*To*
*Mom and Dad*

*To*
*My children,*
*Who make everything worthwhile,*
*Lee, Laurie, Peggy*

*To*
*Jennie*
*And her willingness to*
*rewrite, correct, and*
*to keep encouraging.*

*To*
*Barb, Doreen, and Winnie*
*for not allowing me to give up.*

*Thank you.*

# Part I

# Body

*We humans are comprised of three parts: spirit, soul and body. He began His work on my body.*

# I
# In The Beginning

*In the beginning was the Word and the Word was with God, and the Word was God. He was in the beginning with God.* (John 1:1-2)

Not me. In the beginning for me was me. And me was not so bad. In fact, me was pretty good. I was positive, accomplished, strong-willed, talented, and vivacious. People liked me and I liked them. I achieved all I set out to achieve with little effort and you often wonder what effort could have brought me.

I have one brother and we grew up in what seems like an idyllic family. Although not "huggers," my parents gave me absolute love. I never heard my mom and dad fight and the first fight my brother and I had was when I was twelve years old. I still remember the terrible feelings I had about it.

Lee and I were much loved and watched over in our busy, protective family of grandparents and parents. My parents worked a family-owned steel stamping business they had built up from a wood working business my great-grandfather had begun. Our family lived that business at all times. On weekends when the family cleaned the shop, I would put on my roller skates, grab a broom and sweep the plant floor around those big presses, past spot welders — Wow, what fun! Never much real work done. I sure learned to skate, though. My brother and I hauled one another in the pulley carts, even though dad and mom had to spend so much time there, we were together.

My Pa. Dutch Grandmother was the one who stayed at home with Lee and me and gave all the hugs and kisses. She filled our tummies with good cooking, our souls with her special grandma love and our spirits with an awareness of God. One of my clearest memories is of the big black leather chair she sat in and her worn Bible sitting on the stand next to it. She also made the best brown sugar cookies. I never knew how hard my parents worked because Grandma and Grandpa McNeal took such good care of us. If God loved me anything like my grandmother did, He had to be all right.

So vivid is the memory when Grandma got sick. I was only ten and could not go into the hospital, but would stand in the parking lot waiting and watching her window for her hand to wave at me, "Oh, Lee, there is her hand. She is O.K. She is waving!" Oh my, how I loved her! Then Mom and Dad told me she had gone to heaven. I wanted to die, too . . . or instead. She was in her coffin in the front room of her home and her hand of love was cold. When everyone left the room I would go back in alone, I held her once warm hand and begged God to bring Grandma back and take me instead. I wasn't all that good and she was and the world needed her. I did not know God like Grandma did, but I sat expecting her eyes to open. I watched her. I waited. I waited. The big tear drops just kept coming. I needed her.

Yet, I knew where she was. She was with the God she loved and the God she shared with us. My parents always sent Lee and me to church with her. One day Lee argued with dad, "if you don't have to go, why do I have to go?" From then on we began to go as a family.

I believed in God and the Christmas story and Easter ones about Jesus, as I would swing on my trapeze that Grandpa built in the trees, staring at the clouds where I thought God lived. I sometimes could see castles and angels, doves — sometimes a cross — maybe a boat like the one Jesus sailed in. Surely that meant He was up there.

I remember around age fourteen, sitting in our little church one Sunday and feeling God tell me He wanted me to be a missionary. At that time everyone knew that God did not talk to anyone; so after a few snickers, I dropped the idea. After all, missionaries went to Africa and I was afraid of spiders, bugs, and all those things.

To this warm heritage was added the teaching of positive thinking. I was brought up to be my own thinker, encouraged by my wonderful parents that *can't* should not be a part of my vocabulary, especially because I was an American. My parents not only talked this way — they lived it! Thus, I was a very assured little girl. My family told me I was just the best they ever did see and I believed them.

In my late teens my self-assuredness mated with my immaturity and produced rebellion. To please my parents I had entered Youngstown University. I was active and accepted, but I thought I knew more what was right for me, so I quit school after one year, as soon as a good job was offered. Money and independence seemed more important than mere school. Added to this budding rebellion was a vulnerability. I had suffered a broken engagement, along with my broken heart, soon after graduation.

This was absolutely the wrong time for Mike to come into my life, but in he came. Mike was a young man I had thought was great in high school. But he never took a second look at me. He had been away in the Navy and was now home. He was used to being his own boss and I was still vulnerable from rejection. My parents saw through to our differences, but I would not. After a few months of going together, marriage was decided upon. My mother begged me to wait to get to know him better. I chose to see what I wanted, how I wanted. When he was jealous of my friends, I thought it was cute; he wanted to spend all his time with me. He quit swearing because it offended my family. He quit smoking because I did not smoke. I thought if he would change for me, that proved he loved me. When he told people he would do whatever was necessary to get me, even if it meant marriage, I was sure that was love. Rebellion distorts perception and wisdom.

While going to church with my family I had learned the Ten Commandments and I knew I should be honoring my parents, but I decidedly pushed everything out of my mind except to have my own way. In total rebellion, we decided to elope. We went to Maryland to be married. On the trip there I was very upset because I had left my parents in a terrible state. I cried most of the way. At one point I heard a voice say very clearly to me, "Do not do this." I looked at Mike with my mouth wide open, thinking he had said it. Seeing that it was not he, I returned to looking out the window. Once again I heard the voice very clearly in a completely normal tone say, "Do not do this." Mike then turned to me very angrily and asked, "Well, you want me to turn around?" I was so startled, I shook my head and we went on to Maryland.

I would learn later to recognize that voice as the Holy Spirit of God. God had spoken to me and given me direction but I had chosen my own path. I knew about God but I was not with God. His Word was with me but I was not following it.

What kind of marriage do you have when you start it in absolute rebellion to the Holy Spirit and your parents? Mike and I soon found out. We had many tough days. We found we had little in common to keep us together. I liked sports. Mike did not. Mike liked a few beers. I hated them. His cigarettes soon reappeared. He liked late nights. I needed to sleep and loved early mornings. Arguments and hurt feelings filled our lives. But so did babies.

We were married one year and had a darling baby boy. Lee Michael was born. He was healthy, intelligent and good. Time began to go faster and two years and four months later, a darling, curly-headed, green-eyed beauty, Laurie Joe, was born to us. Then in another two years and four months, our dark-haired, brown-eyed baby doll, Peggy Jane, arrived.

One thing I had insisted on before we were married was that since Mike did not have a church, he would go with me. He had agreed, but now he would not. Faithfully each Sunday I took the children, but the man who appeared to change for me before marriage would not fulfill what he had promised. When I asked him why, his answer was, "Oh, I knew if I told you that, you would marry me. See how much I love you?" But now that was not ringing true. Inside, I felt like I belonged to God, but I did not know how far I was from Him. I did not know that in the Bible in Deuteronomy 28, we can choose blessings or cursings and that can influence our lives and our children. I did not know that my choice of rebellion had sown the seeds of cursing, as a crisis was to enter my life when Peggy was just a baby. Through it I would know God's hand on my life in a way that I never knew was possible and He would begin to turn me from the path rebellion had chosen.

**Helen & Bill Radler**

**Grandpa & Grandma McNeal with Linda**

**Mom — Linda, new brother Lee**

**Linda & Lee on trapeze**

Lee & Linda

Laurie, Lee & baby Peggy

Linda, Helen, Lee & Bill Radler

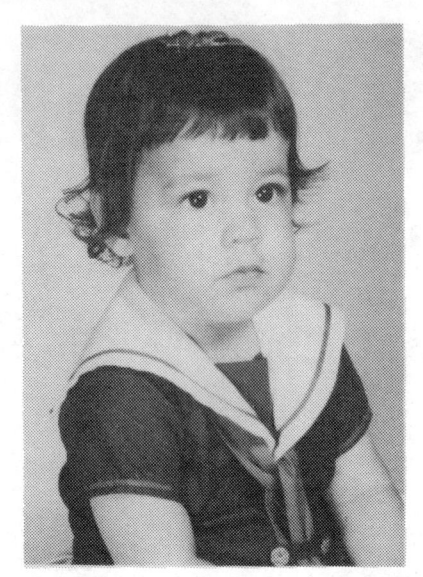

**Peggy Jane**

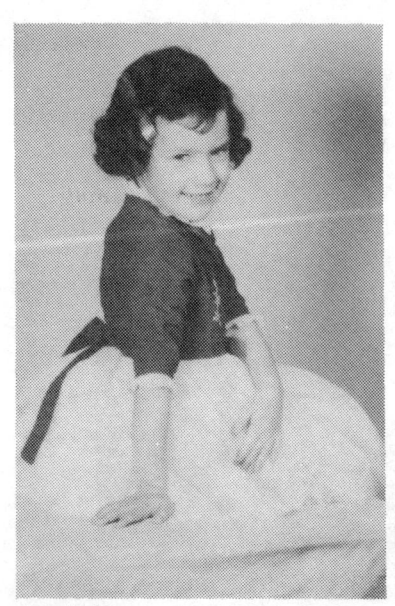

**Laurie Jo**

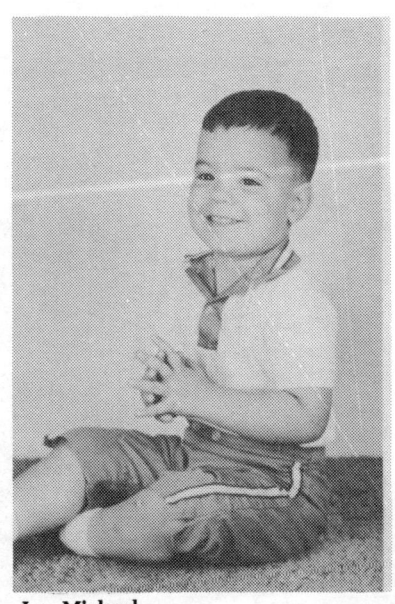

**Lee Michael**

# II
# Epilepsy?
# No, Not Me!

It was early morning. I was at the ironing board and Mike was in the bathroom yelling because I should have had his shirt ironed before he needed it. Abruptly, this so familiar scene changed. I awoke hours later with my family and doctor surrounding me. My jaws and muscles ached from what had gripped me. I had no consciousness of what I had done during those hours. My family described to me the contortions of my head banging against the floor, the ridged jerking and convulsing of my body. My entire being had been out of control. The trauma of this transgression overwhelmed me. My doctor insisted we find out the cause.

Days later I sat in the specialist's office, my mind going in so many directions. I knew something was wrong; but not this. **Not Epilepsy!** Me, an epileptic? Those people who jerked and convulsed and bit their tongues? NO! NO. It could not be! It was the disease that the maniac had in the Bible, the disease that Jesus cast out of the young man, the disease that people shied away from. NO! NO! I knew it was said to be inherited, but I could think of no one in my family who had it.

"Linda," the doctor interrupted my thoughts, "we are just finding out so much about this disease, that it is not always inherited and that a severe blow to the head can cause it."

Remembering back, I was twelve years old when one of the neighbors had thrown those big black walnuts with their hard green coverings at us kids, teasing us to get on home. I was scared and had hidden behind one of the big trees. When all got quiet I peeked out. Whack! A walnut hit me between the eyes knocking me almost cold. Then at fourteen I began every once in a while to have these funny feelings like I might black out, but I never quite did.

By the time I was a senior in high school, I was passing out more frequently; however, I was otherwise healthy. I was head majorette, played clarinet, played basketball, swam, roller-skated, and seldom missed a day of school.

Epilepsy! I was back in the doctor's office listening to his instructions. There was no cure for this disease, but they could control it pretty well with certain drugs. I was to start on them right away and be turned over to my family physician. Fighting back tears, suddenly I felt guilty, embarrassed, afraid. Would people think I was crazy? What about my family? All these thoughts and feelings were there and more. Fear gripped me. Oh God! Why did you do this to me?

I began to live with my epilepsy. With medication I would still have seizures, but they were further apart. Yet when I had them they were stronger. As they became stronger, they became more fearful to me and everyone around. They could happen at any time, anywhere. It was a feeling of something coming up from my feet like warm water and as it got to my lungs I began to gasp for breath. I felt as if I were being suffocated. A terrific fear set in and I would fight this feeling with every ounce of resistance I could muster. Then it closed over my head and I would black out. All this happened in a few seconds. Sometimes I would wake and a crowd would be around me and sometimes I would be all alone. But the worst was to wake with my children bending over me crying, "Mommy, wake up, Mommy!"

Seizures sometimes came when I would sense an odd odor that only I experienced. But more often I would sense that I had been in this place or time before and a seizure would come. I began to hear about ESP and some kind of meditation and reincarnation. I wondered if I could be affected by these things. Unknown to me then, the nature of my disease made me susceptible to the ESP and reincarnation teachings. Because I seemed to know before-hand places and things, I accepted the idea that I could have lived before. It was not hard for me to believe I had great spiritual qualities. I had a real affinity for Egypt and the pyramids. I felt that if I had lived before I was probably Egyptian. I was absorbed with archaeology and thoughts of life-past. Although I could not fit this in with the Christianity I was brought up with, I felt part of two worlds.

Changes in our life kept me from having time to be deeply involved with these ideas. Mike got a job in the strip mines in southern Ohio as a welder on the largest mining shovel built, ironically named the Gem of Egypt. We packed up children and furniture and took off for southern Ohio. We tried to rent a home but had no success. Finally, we found a new house that we could buy on land contract. Later I would know we were moved there for a purpose. Our home was on top of the ridge and the view was fantastic. It was in a new section of homes and there were many families around our age and our children's ages. I never had any trouble making friends, so I became busy with being busy . . . church, choir, cub scouts, little league, PTA, 4-H, etc. I was still having seizures and trying to fight them. No one there knew I was an epileptic and I was not about to tell them either.

I was told that one of the neighbors was very religious and I thought, "Oh, well, so am I." But I did notice something a bit different about the family and I really liked them. She invited me to her church and mentioned the word in conversation of being "saved." This was the first time that I had heard that in connection with good attendance at church. Good, polite, church-goer that I was, I said, "Oh, that is nice." But I was not about to let her know that I had no idea what she was talking about. I smiled and nodded and just went on with the conversation. But it was funny how that one word "saved" seemed to affect me.

Mike was working many hours trying to complete the schedule for the shovel and this was good for us. We did not see much of each other and things were going well for us financially, so there was little fighting which was an unusual and pleasant relief.

Yet, there were to be complications in our lives that would be overwhelming.

# III
# His Hand Of Mercy

Early one warm June evening in 1967, just about dark, I received a phone call. It was Mike. He sounded strange and told me there had been an accident. He had stepped off his monstrous truck and had broken his ankle and would I please come to Barnesville to get him. The doctor then came on the phone and said for me to come to the hospital; they were getting ready to set his ankle and I should be there.

I hung up the phone and my mind started to race. What about the kids? Get my clothes changed. Then, suddenly, the realization, "in Barnesville!" I had no idea where that was. I called my neighbor whose husband also worked night turn. She said not to worry that we would just pile the kids in the car and find Barnesville. She had lived in the area all her life and knew Barnesville was about forty miles away but had never been there. I could not find a map and was frantic to get started. We decided it must be down river and that is the direction we started out. Quite a number of miles later we found an open gas station but no one there knew how to get to Barnesville either. Finally, we found a station where we were given directions. We were heading south all right but Barnesville was southwest and we were heading southeast. A one hour trip took us more than two hours and it seemed like twelve.

At last we arrived. The children, her four and my three, were all packed in the back of the station wagon tired and sleepy. I had prayed but realized that I was not sure He even heard me. I rushed through the hospital door into the empty waiting room. As I approached the desk for directions an orderly asked if I were Mrs. Gregorino. At that moment I knew it was worse than I had expected. He saw my face and began to tell me that

Mike was okay. He was alive, would be okay, but the doctor wanted to see me.

The doctor explained that they not only had to set Mike's ankle but it required some surgery. He continued that the accident had been serious, but he knew I wanted to see Mike and would explain more later. He cautioned me not to be shocked, for Mike was still affected by the anesthetic and was also in shock.

"Okay," I thought, "I'm ready. Just let me see him." But I was not ready. As I walked in, he was delirious and hollering, "Please don't let my leg be off!" he pleaded. "Please look and see if it is still there!" He recognized me for just a minute and became quiet while I took a look at him. He was covered with cuts and bruises, dirt was still in his hair and eyes, small pieces of shattered glass was all over him, a huge gash was on his right forearm and the left elbow looked as if nothing was left but raw hamburger. I took a wash cloth to wipe his face but he began to scream, "Get out of the way, get out of the way!" Then again the cry, "See if my leg is still there!"

The leg was still there but in a cast. The doctor came in and explained a bit more about the surgery. Mike's ankle was shattered and they had had to insert metal screws to hold the foot on the leg. His elbow was badly damaged and the ulna nerve was almost severed. It would take time, but it would eventually grow together, yet there was no promise that there would not be some permanent damage.

My mind whirled. What could have possibly happened to cause this? The doctor assured me that Mike's foreman would return to the hospital and explain the accident to me. They gave Mike medication to ease the pain and help him sleep. He pleaded for me to stay and I promised to be with him. I went to the car and told my friend to go home, this was going to be a long night, and asked her to call my parents to come and take the children to come to stay with them.

I was in Barnesville. I didn't know how I arrived because of the roundabout way we had come. There I was with a husband in serious condition and I had no idea how it had happened. There I was, realizing I had no way home. I had no car. I knew not one person. What a feeling! God was out there somewhere. I hoped He was not too far away to hear me. Yet even at this point of faith, there was comfort that I believed in

Him.

As I went back to Mike's room he, in his delirium, was reliving the accident. Over and over he screamed, "Look out! Look out! Get the radio! Watch the dozer!" Then again and again, "Oh, God, please let my leg be there! Look! Look! See if it's still there!" Hour after hour he called on God to save his leg, promising, always promising, to go to church if God would just save his leg. I tried to reassure him that his leg was there, but he was not conscious enough to hear me.

Finally, his foreman arrived and began to put the pieces together for me. He related that they knew Mike was in trouble when Mike called on the radio for them to clear the ramp. His truck was free-wheeling and he had no brakes. From the top of the ramp the foreman and others had watched as the truck went faster and faster down the incline, then as it exploded, they saw what they thought was Mike jumping from the cab. The truck had continued, hit a dip, turned on end, then come to a rest on its wheels as it hit a dirt pile. All operations stopped as they searched in the dark for Mike. They could not believe that he was alive. A doctor was a visitor at the mine that night and when he heard the call come over the radio, he came to help. He stopped the men from cutting off Mike's boot which helped keep the foot and ankle immobilized until he got to the hospital. He also gave Mike a pain shot immediately which helped him to be able to call me and sound so calm.

That entire night and most of the next day Mike would ride that truck down that hill every twenty minutes or so and cry out, "Please, God, let my leg be there!" As Mike became more rational, he began to relate the story of his nightmare. A ramp in the strip mine was actually only a mound of dirt with large pieces of slag formed into a narrow incline that resulted in a slippery track of clay with sheer drops on either side. As Mike had started down the ramp he realized that his brakes were not holding. Then the clutch engaged and caused the motor to blow up. The cab filled with smoke and as Mike reached to return the radio mike a piece of metal cut a gash across his arm. Trying to see and not to hit a dozer operator who might be on the ramp, Mike stuck his head out the cab window. As he put his head out, the flywheel blew up from the floor, whizzing past the place where Mike's head would have been and cut through the roof of the cab. As metal cut metal, small pieces flew all over the cab, cutting Mike. Then as hot oil began to spray over everything, the opposite door of the cab blew off. Mike knew in a split second it was jump or be crushed to death. By now the speed of the truck had reached nearly seventy miles per hour because of the push of the coal in the bed behind him. In the midst of all this, Mike had the presence of mind to think, "I have to hold my head up so those big pieces of slag won't cut my face." Jump he did, putting his left hand up under his chin trying to protect his face. When he landed, his feet hit first and his ankle was crushed. He then fell on his elbow, which was why it was so mangled. But it did protect his face. Mike tried to get up and walk. His only thoughts at this time were of another truck coming down the ramp and running over him because of the darkness. His leg just would not walk for him, so he started wiggling to the ramp edge. A dozer operator who had seen it all from the top of the ramp was the first person to reach Mike, making him lie down.

Many said Mike was lucky. I say there were too many coincidences to be luck. Mike's mind was too collected and calm not to recognize God in this. People say it is in these desperate situations that bravery shows up. I agree, but both Mike and I knew he was not that brave and not at all that kind of calm. When we face crises like this, we know the courage that we have is not from ourselves, but from God.

This was the first time Mike was ever in a hospital as a patient and he gave the nurses and me fits. He was required to learn to use crutches before he was allowed to go home. Mike was insistent and persistent and in less than a week after the accident the doctor relented and released him if I were willing to care for him at home. I felt I could care for him fine, and it would be better than all those miles of driving every day. I was wrong!

It was hot and the cast made Mike sweat and itch. he could not use the crutches effectively because of the damage to his elbow and his grip on the left hand was very bad. He could not sleep well because of the nightmares. Then, during the day, he would get so frustrated to be outside that he would crawl out the door. We finally fixed up the riding lawn mower so he could get on it and prop his leg and drive around to visit neighbors and relieve some of the boredom.

But Mike's misery was not all physical. He was not pleased

with God and would say so. I would remind him of his promises to God while in the hospital and he would give me a look that told me my timing was wrong. He began to tell me he wasn't even sure he believed in God. But I heard him call to God to save his leg and I knew somewhere inside was an empty place that was crying for God. I, too, was searching for more truth because in my mind and heart I knew God had spared Mike's life. Mike had put his promise somewhere in the back of his mind, but I had a little more trouble in doing this.

Mike was in a cast for twelve weeks. His ankle was left with some stiffness and weather conditions could make him limp painfully. His arm took longer to regain strength, but finally he was back to work. I would ask him to go to church with us and he would fly into a rage. "How could I ask him to do this when this was his only day off and after all he had just had a terrible accident and had almost lost his leg! He needed his rest!"

In some ways, I can understand why Mike did not want to go. I left my religion at church on Sunday and went back the next Sunday to pick it up. I thought that was certainly all God required of me, to do good deeds, help people — which I loved doing, anyway, for the doing of it made me feel good, not knowing how to do deeds in the love of God. There is a word used in the Bible — *pious* — that word fit me, although I would have been very angry if anyone had said that about me. I did not understand God and true Christianity. I wanted to. The Lord had touched my life. He knew I had a heart to love Him and He would faithfully continue to touch my life and reveal Himself to me. I was tired of being ill. Why was my physical body falling apart? I was about to have the light of Jesus begin to open some dark places inside of me. Willfulness and rebellion had turned us to go our own way. But God in His mercy toward His creation would take His hand and begin leading through the confusion of the detour that had been chosen. I would soon come to a place of desperation.

# IV
# Help Comes

My epileptic seizures were still plaguing me and now that we lived in an area where there was heavy pollution, my yearly summer hay fever turned to asthma. Every time the pollution went up I had to go into the hospital for oxygen and adrenalin. I was finally started on allergy injections. During that winter I became very ill with a high fever and was delirious for three days. Mike did not realize how sick I was and I just had to keep going. Finally, I just could not drag myself out of bed. My parents came for a visit, took one look at me, and said, "She's going to the hospital."

The hospital did not know what was wrong with me except that I had a very high fever and could not breathe. The fever persisted for almost seven days. I was put in a room with a lady who smoked and she would fall asleep and set her bed on fire. They would take her cigarettes away from her, but she always got more. What a situation! I was too weak by this time to get out of bed, my chest would burn like fire when she smoked, and to relieve some of the chest pain, they gave me a drug called Talwin. I had an immediate and overwhelming reaction to this drug. I began hallucinating, my bed was floating in the middle of water. All I could see was water and my bed was rocking and weaving. And this was no dream, I was awake! Every once in a while in the far distance I would see a person who looked like a nurse pass by and I would call for help, but she could not get to me because of the water. One of the nurses was a neighbor and I would call, "Joyce, tell them to come and get me." Then the room would explode into wild colors so bright that they hurt my eyes. To put it mildly, I was frightened. They had to tie me to the bed until the drug wore off.

There I was with cigarette smoke suffocating me and my mind out of control. I was almost to the point that my chest hurt so when I tried to breathe that I thought it would just be easier to not breathe any more. My family saw me getting worse and worse and insisted that I be transferred to my doctor nearer home, who had taken care of me and my children. In two days I was much improved. As he treated my asthma, my chest problem cleared up and finally the fever left. On one of my frequent check-up trips the doctor asked if he had ever mentioned a heart murmur before. I said, no, not even through the birth of three children. He said He would keep a check on it — that it was probably nothing. I had begun to notice a shortness of breath, but we all thought it was connected with the asthma.

At last summer came. We were getting back on our feet physically and financially. It had been a year since Mike's accident. His temper was getting worse and the worse his temper got, the more I would just grab the children up and leave the house, telling him he'd better get to church.

I became good friends with a new neighbor who had come to this country from Germany. Kris was the nicest person and what a story she had about escaping from the Russians in East Germany. I was fascinated by the things she and her family had been through. One Sunday afternoon she came over and told me that she was so happy that her husband got "saved." Now her whole family had gone to the altar. There was that word again. I said, "Oh, that's nice, that's good, aren't you happy?" But in my mind I was thinking, "Saved! What does she mean, saved? I'm good. What do I need to be saved from?" Strange, isn't it, that when a word has power from God, it makes you feel uncomfortable and you put up all kinds of barriers. But God recognizes no barriers.

One summer evening when the children were all out playing and Mike was at work, I turned on the T.V. A Billy Graham Crusade was on and I did not change the channel. I thought he was a little fanatical, but he said, "God does not change to suit us. He is the same as He has been and will be." I did not know that. I thought He did things in Bible times and now He did not. He just left us to make our own way. That night I watched the whole program and cried, cried, and cried. There was the word again, "saved." I was not going to be a fanatic, but the second night I watched the program again with the same sensation and tears. I turned it off quickly. That was enough of that! The next evening I had worked in the yard and came into the house very hot and tired. Grabbed a pop, flipped on T.V. — we had a T.V. that took a while to warm up, so I propped up my feet, and Oh, brother! It was him again. I thought I'm too tired to move. It must be almost over. I did not know he was on three nights in a row. I was weeping in front of the T.V. in spite of myself. I thought if I would just do what he said — kneel by the television and pray with him, then maybe all of this would quit.

I prayed with Billy Graham and asked Jesus to come into my heart. There were no grand feelings — only my weeping did stop and I felt so very good. Now, you must know that I was not about to tell anyone what I had done. After all, I was a good church person. No one in my church had ever told me about a salvation experience. What would they think of me?

My epileptic seizures seemed to stay far apart, but they were not easy. I would feel the curse of this disease begin to come over me and I would be gripped, encompassed, paralyzed with fear. Oh, how I hated it. This was not me. I was repulsed by it and sick that as others saw this tormented being they would think it was me. It came upon me, overtook me. I wanted no one — especially my children — to be exposed to this. Fear and panic raged through me, but I had no control.

Just two weeks after I had prayed with Billy Graham, I was standing in the kitchen frying french fries for the children, when I felt a seizure coming. I grabbed for the hot oil, panicked at the thought of fire; I got it off the burner, grabbed onto the sink fighting with all I had against this thing, having tried to fight it so many times before and knowing I would lose. I raised my fist up toward the ceiling, hollering, "Jesus, help! If you really are real and any of this is true that I heard about you on T.V., please help me!"

Just before that terrible feeling of suffocation took over, a cool, soothing inner shower washed over me and drained out my feet. The seizure had left as quickly as it had come. I stood there hanging onto the sink, shaking my head in disbelief. I had to sit down on the floor. I sat crying and laughing, totally surprised. I had believed in God for as long as I can remember and believed that Jesus was His Son, but to find out He was close enough for me to call and He would answer was overwhelming. Jesus was really real. He was not on a cloud somewhere, not millions of miles away, not too busy to hear me call. He had sent me power to fight. My mind was boggled, healing was supposed to be in days past. The children began to fuss, "Mommy, do our french fries! We're hungry! Get up off the floor!" I began to laugh. I did not know what had happened, but I was going to find out.

I went over and over in my mind what had happened. I knew something happened when I cried, "Jesus!" But who could I tell and what would they say if I did? I kept quiet. As an epileptic, you never confessed to anyone that you had it, so how could I ever explain this? But I knew that God had touched me when I went to Him through the name of His Son, Jesus.

Have you ever driven over a rutty road where you drive off trying to miss a hole and then get back on and slow down and speed up? That is just what I seemed to do next. As I would remember to call on the name of Jesus and fight those seizures, they would pass. But if I began to think it was all in my head and doubt, that old fear would come and I would have a seizure. Over the next six months I learned to fight the fear that old sluefoot puts on an epileptic and as I began to trust in the name of Jesus, my seizures became further and less and less powerful. I began to forget to take my medication, dilantin, and after one year realized I did not need it at all. This is when I began to realize that even though it is not supposed to happen, I had been healed of epilepsy.

We had applied for a new hospitalization policy. Since I believed my epilepsy to be gone, I did not record having it. When the insurance company checked our records, they said I was an epileptic and trying to deceive them. We retained an attorney because we needed our policy to pay a bill and in order to prove our case, I was sent to a hospital for a new EEG. The doctor who read the test results said that my brainwaves were normal and that I probably never had epilepsy, for it is a permanent disease. The insurance company relented to pay the hospital bill since the doctor verified that I was not epileptic, but they suggested that we find another company to insure me.

God's mercy had been so great toward me, yet I never once

thought to thank Him. I still had a lot of religion and no deep personal knowledge of Christ. But I did know that I had been touched by the Lord and I had a happiness inside that was always there for me to draw on. Because I was still afraid of what people would think, I would tell no one, but I knew. The Bible began to open up to me.

What Billy Graham said was coming true. I had asked the Lord Jesus into my heart and the Bible was becoming the Living Word. I thought I was a really good person. I would not have changed me, but something was changing me. I had been "saved"! Saved from what? Mostly me. I realize now that I had truly embraced thoughts of reincarnation, that I had opened the door of the occult. Now it was closed. I felt the release from double-mindedness. I could see the road that led to home. But as in all our lives there were situations I could not foresee.

# V
# Dream House

We moved from our new house into an 86 year old farmhouse settled on a few acres of land in East Springfield, Ohio. I was really happy with our purchase. I have been a farm girl at heart from the days back on my grandfather's farm. I love the memories in old things and history has always been one of my interests. I was very happy with my ten room house, its two interesting old winding staircases with large bay windows and huge rooms. Although the porch was falling off and the barn was very old I could see the possibilities in the place. I loved its wonderfully earthy smell of hay and cows, the beautiful woods and its creek and springs bursting forth from the ground seemed to be made just for me. If a place could be your happiness, this was my place. I would walk the woods and pasture, and would sit by the creek and watch the cattle. A new calmness and joy arose in me. I would be overwhelmed by the beauty I saw; I would cry and thank God for this earth. I could not comprehend that God's original earth was even more wonderful than I thought this one is. I was helped by the Lord to begin to let go of grudges and to forgive some of the terrible things Mike's temper was causing him to do. People would ask how I could be so happy. I really could not give them the answer, but God was preparing me for the day I would be able to tell them.

In the midst of this calm came another storm. I began to have trouble with my right arm and some days could not use it because of swelling and pain. I constantly dropped things. Then for a time it would all go away. I was also experiencing shortness of breath continually. Finally my arm got so severe that it would get cold and turn blue and I was learning to eat left-handed. The doctor put me in the hospital looking for a tumor and running various tests including a muscle biopsy. The tests were negative but the severe pain and swelling were most positively still there.

Then one doctor asked if anyone had ever heard a heart murmur before. I acknowledged there had been a suspicion of one before. Arrangements were then made for me to go to the Cleveland Clinic where I went through more neurological tests, more biopsys, and finally they took a piece of nerve out of my leg. None of these tests were conclusive, but one day they arrived in my room to announce that I had a heart problem and would need surgery soon.

Floored! Yes, floored would be the right word. They told me the shortness of breath was my heart most of the time and not asthma. Many nights I could not lie flat to sleep and often I would need to take two or three breaks while walking up the hill behind our house, but we always thought it was the asthma. Heart trouble was unbelievable. And still they had not been able to fully say what was wrong with my arm.

I was sent home in a similar condition to my husband's a few years earlier. I was on crutches from the nerve surgery and could not put my foot down because the stretching of the muscles in my calf caused my leg to hurt terribly but using the crutches made the swelling in my arm worse.

Directly across the road from our farm was a little church which the children and I began to attend. I did not get to know the minister very well before all this happened to me but he came to visit and pray with me after I came home. This was the first time that someone held my hand while they prayed for me and I could feel something going from his hand to mine like current. I actually felt the power of the Lord coming through another person. As he began to pray the day was overcast and in the middle of his prayer sunlight beamed through my big bay window so that even with our eyes closed we knew the sun came out. He looked at his hand, I looked at mine. I cried and he cried. Then he laughed and I laughed. It surprised us both. I felt stronger after his prayer. That day would be forever imprinted in my mind as the assurance of God's presence with me.

Soon it was hay baling time on the farm, time to really work.

Mike was working all daylight shift and driving fifty miles one way to work. This did not give us many hours to get hay in. Our neighbor baled our back field and we were hoping for a good Saturday to finish. We had not been able to round up any extra help so we had only Mike, Lee and me. As we awoke Saturday morning, it was very dark and threatening. It looked as though it were just waiting until we walked out the door to rain. I did the hauling and Mike did the loading. We got a little more than half of the field into the barn when it started to mist, so I began to help with the loading, too. We were working like crazy and my heart was feeling like it was going to explode. We could see the rain coming now over the ridge toward the field.

Out of pure frustration Mike began to yell at Lee and me. I started to cry. Why was he hollering at us? We were working as fast as we could go. My heart felt so tight, it hurt so much. I was near total exhaustion. Mike was taking his anger out on us. Who was I going to take mine out on? I shook my fist to heaven and cried, "Jesus, how can you do this to us?!" Inside, I really felt that God was going to let me have a heart attack and everything would be ruined. I cried, "Help us, Lord!" The rain came to the fence. We could see it bouncing from the fence posts. Yet in our field it was only misting. As we took the last load safely into the barn the rain moved in sheets across our field. In the barn it sounded like the wind would take the roof off.

The minute I got into the barn I knew I had falsely accused God. I asked the Lord to forgive me for thinking that He wanted to hurt us in any way. I was just beginning to learn about God's love and His true ways. I had for so long just known what others told me they thought He was like, that I was constantly having to change my thinking to His revelation of Himself now that He lived within me. I knew I deserved His wrath because I seemed to be blaming Him unnecessarily, butHe chose what humbled me and brought Him glory. He chose to pour forth His grace and hold back the rain. I will not forget that day. Later as I was reading in Psalms I found this verse, "He caused the storm to be still, so that the waves of it were hushed. Then they were glad because they were quiet; So He guided them to their desired haven." (Psalms 107:29-30 NAS) Again Jesus was making the Word alive for me. I had actually experienced what the Bible spoke.

My shortness of breath continued to get worse. I could no longer sleep lying down at all. I would sit and hold my arm and cry and cry. Nothing could reach the pain; it was there all the time now. It had begun to localize in my elbow, shoulder, wrist and was beginning in my knees. I could not get sufficient rest because of this double problem and it was beginning to tell on me. My family physician decided to have a second opinion on my heart, and sent me to Akron, Ohio for testing. While there they did more tests on my arm. They confirmed I had rheumatic heart disease. Mitral stenosis was the term which meant that my heart valve was narrowing. They thought maybe the joint pain was a related form of the rheumatic fever. I had all the symptoms of a couple of serious muscle or joint diseases. They decided to treat the symptoms to try to give me some relief, even though the disease could not be absolutely diagnosed. I began a program of cortizone. The relief was immediate. I had been so long with this pain that my gratitude overflowed. But it was short lived as the cortizone affected my kidneys drastically. I was taken off cortizone and told, "Linda, you will have to learn to live with the pain." What a prospect!

When I left the hospital this time I was to return in two months for a cardiac catherization which would tell the heart doctor how much damage was done in my heart and how much surgery was required. This was scheduled for the month of August, 1972. They told me to prepare my family and my household for the operation. This was frightening, for I knew that the possibility of death was there. Just as the valve in my heart was narrowing, so my life and faith seemed to narrow. Yet God had turned me toward Himself. His hand was upon me and He would let me know Him.

# VI
# Heart Surgery

While waiting for my heart surgery we got our steers and heifers ready for the fairs and traveled to a few county fairs and the Ohio State Fair. We returned in time for a Lay Witness Mission at our church. I did not know what a Lay Mission was, but it sounded good and it was. As a follow up to the mission, a group of young fellows called the "Young Apostles" were brought to the church to minister to our young people in song. Judge Spon, a local Christian attorney and judge, had helped in getting this group to my church. This was the first time I had heard anything quite that loud in a church, especially that bunch of drums! My thoughts were that they were not reverent enough for me and surely God was holding His ears. But when they were through witnessing and praising the Lord, I was enjoying them as much as anyone. I had grown up in churches and had heard many good sermons, but never had I heard anyone just include Jesus and the Holy Spirit in their conversation the way these young men did. To speak the name of Jesus was just as natural to them as it was for me to say coffee or tea. I liked it, but I knew that I was unable to do this.

A young man named Bob stood up and wanted to tell us what Jesus had done for him. My first reaction was, "My goodness, he better get some more done!" He had hair down to his shoulders, both front teeth were gone and every place that you could see any skin had a tatoo on it. He began to tell us that he had been in the "Hell's Angels" motorcycle gang and some of the things he had done and how he had been addicted to drugs. Then he told us he had asked the Lord to come into his heart and how much Jesus had done for him. I forgot all about the tatoos and hair and got excited. This was what I needed to hear.

He gave the first altar call I had ever heard that was "in person." I was there. I could respond and others could see me. I later found out this was called public confession. A young girl had responded and was weeping. I kept thinking someone should go stand with her, not leave her up there all alone. Before I knew what had happened, I was standing with her, hugging her. I do not remember moving from my seat. The rest of the young people were then asked to come forward and to let Bob pray with them. I watched as all three of mine found a place at the altar. I was so happy!

I returned to my seat as the service was over except for the prayer. Then our choir director asked for special prayer for me because I was going to have heart surgery in two days. I was kind of surprised, but thought that that was really nice. I thought I would just sit there in my back pew and they would pray, but they called me down front. What could I do, but to go down front? Bob asked me to kneel. This was getting a little embarrassing, really, twice in one day, but I could not make a scene. I knelt down, not willingly, with the thoughts in my head going many different directions! "Fanatical, but this was in the Bible." "Embarrassing, but they did it because they care." "Why me?" Then with his tatoos, scars and long hair, Bob laid his hands on my head and prayed. I would never be the same again! I did not hear one word he was praying for me because that same electricity I felt when our pastor had prayed for me months earlier was running all through me. I did not understand, but practically floated out of church that day. I was so excited I could not eat dinner. I had to go for a walk down by the creek, then I felt so good I began to walk the fence around the farm and before I knew it, I was back at the house. I was hardly puffing! My husband said I looked like a nut and I probably did since all I could do was grin and my eyes kept watering, not as in crying, just like spigots that have a leak. Mike thought I had flipped and quickly informed me what he thought of my experience, warning me not to speak to him about it again.

One of the neighbors who was in the service when they prayed for me came to the house and gave me a tract. It was all about the healing power of God. I read it and reread it and found much comfort in it. I looked all the Scriptures up to be sure they were really in the Bible. It was published by some group I had never heard of, the Full Gospel Businessmen. In fact, this was the first tract I had ever seen. Then our new minister came to see me. He said not to read that stuff, to burn it. I did not see anything wrong with it. It made me feel like there was hope. But, good, faithful, church-member that I was, I burned it. Then I decided that if God wanted me healed, that was fine, I would appreciate it, but I would gladly be a Joan of Arc for Him. After all, I could certainly suffer for Him, considering how much He had done for me! Now I know that was just my pride showing; it did not impress God one little bit. I needed to find out I could not do Him any great favors. He had already sent Jesus to do them for me. But such was my state as I went in for surgery.

The couple of days before the surgery were spent in being told what to expect upon waking and practicing on a machine that was to help me breathe and learning not to fight it. I tried not to think about the actual surgery. But I was really scared. The Lord had touched me enough times that I believed it was going to be all right and all my upbringing was to always be positive, and this was a place where all was working for my good, and I knew many people were praying for me. I was really up early the morning of surgery. I was beginning to get a few butterflies. They gave me a shot to relax me, but I had had so many of these that it did not have the normal effect on me. My family was there trying to be cheerful; but no one could talk very much without crying, so we just smiled at each other a lot. I felt for them. They were going to have a rougher time during the next four hours of conscious wondering than I would in unconsciousness. I was lying there, wanting the gurney to come and take me to surgery and get it over with and yet not really wanting it all to happen either.

Finally they came, everyone telling everyone not to worry. At the elevator door it finally hit me that that may have been the last time I would see my family. As we went into the elevator an amazing thing happened to me. The most wonderful peace just seemed to cover over me like a huge blanket. It is very hard to describe. But it was another one of those feelings that stay with you forever after. I felt peace, love, gentleness and an overwhelming assurance that all was well. Normally, my heart would be racing, my mouth dry, and I would be thinking of all the things I should have done. What I was thinking was, what is this feeling? Then there was someone at my head looking down at me. He just peeked over the top of my head right into my face. He was olive-skinned, had dark hair and a mustache and the most sparkling dark eyes I had ever seen. Very quietly he asked, "Are you prepared?"

I said, "Yes."

He asked, "Are you right with Jesus?"

I said, "Yes."

He asked, "Is He in your heart?"

I said, "Yes," and at the minute the elevator door opened I was wheeled out of the elevator into surgery. I turned to take another look at this special man, but no one looking like him was there.

The nurse asked if they had forgotten to give me my shot because I was so wide awake. I assured her they had given it to me. I heard a lot of people coming into the room and I asked what was happening. They told me that I was going to be observed because my case was a "textbook case." I thought I should pray but could not think of one word except the Twenty-third Psalm that some dear teacher made me memorize in Sunday School. That is what I was saying as I went to sleep . . . even if I walk through the valley of the shadow of death . . .

The next memory I have is of the nurse calling me and telling me I had visitors for just a minute. I do not remember too much except the look on Mike's face when he saw me. He was trying to be so brave. I had tubes out my nose, out my mouth, out of each arm, and out my side. Mike said, "Hi, Honey, we are here." I could see big tears form in his eyes. Reverend Hubbard was with him. He told me I was going to be just fine, then he comforted Mike as they walked away. My Mom and Dad just could not look at me, and it is no wonder.

The days before surgery they spent teaching me to breathe on the machine were good, for I was not able to breathe on my own. However, I am a person who has trouble just gargling and I knew that the tube down my throat was going to be one of my biggest problems. As I became more awake, I would keep gagging. Again I would think of the Twenty-third Psalm and it would calm me and I would usually doze off right away.

Day and night became one for me for a while, but the day

after surgery, I think, a nurse said, "Mrs. Gregorino, we are going to change your bed and you need to get up and sit in the chair."

I said, "Ha! Ha! You're kidding! You don't know what they did to me!"

She smiled and said, "You can make it." I thought they were wild. I was not even sure I was all there to be moved because I hurt so bad. But up we got and I am sure the chair was at least two miles away from the bed. However, I did make it to the chair with two bags, two bottles and numerous wires attached to me.

My surgeon said it was a beautiful textbook case all the way, as he patted my toes. That did not make me feel any better at all; I hurt all over. He said that they did not have to replace the valve, just remove some scar tissue. He was very pleased with me.

After four weeks I finally went home. The kids could hardly believe it was me after this much time. I looked much different to them. Peggy, the youngest, took it quite hard. She even had difficulty sitting on my lap. She felt I had deserted her and did not want to come home. The others felt if they hugged me too hard I would split open. My eyes were opened to how children might feel in a situation like this. How I wish I had realized the pain I was in caused me to look toward myself, not realizing how much they loved me and if I had taken more time to explain and prepare them, they would not have had to suffer and fear unnecessarily.

People were great from my church. They had a schedule set up with food coming from everywhere for each meal. What a help that was! My Mother came to stay with us until I got stronger. I was not allowed to climb stairs more than once a day and at first I could not make it that much.

While recuperating, I had a lot of time to think and wonder about that feeling of peace I had in the elevator. When I asked Jesus what it was He answered, "Prayers." WOW! Even now I still wonder about that man who peered into my face and asked if I was ready. Could he have been an angel? I may never truly know about him, but I truly know that the presence of God enveloped me. But there was yet a closeness to come of which I knew nothing at this point.

# VII
# Even When Walking Through the Dark Valley
## Psalm 23:4

Mother went home after one week, needing to get back to help Dad with the office work and with my assurance that I could handle it. But after one day on my own, I was exhausted, and I told Mike when he got home that he would just have to get his own dinner and take care of the kids. He exploded, "I have to work all day and drive all the way home and take care of all the rest, too? Well, I wish you would have died. It would be a lot easier."

That I was not prepared for. My heart did a flip and went out of time, racing faster and faster. I was becoming very short of breath. My heart could not right itself back to regular rhythm. This is called cardiac arrhythmia.

We were about ninety-five miles from the hospital. We called the doctor and he told us to get there immediately. They rushed me back to the Akron hospital where I was put in coronary care for four days hooked up again to the bottles and machines. After the fourth day I seemed to be stabilized once more. They decided to move me to the Sixth Floor, where I had just spent the four weeks after surgery. By this time the CCU nurses and the Sixth Floor people knew me pretty well. The doctor kept saying, I just don't see how this happened. I decided I would say nothing. Surely Mike did not mean what he had said. I determined I would forgive him and forget it. I did what I prayed so often. I forgave so that I could be forgiven (The Lord's Prayer). At this time I did not realize the power in forgiveness, but that determination kept that wonderful joy flowing in my life.. When we obey the instructions Jesus gave us whether we know exactly what we do or not, God moves.

As they moved me and my bed to the Sixth Floor and one of the CCU nurses came along with me, I thought she was walking along to make sure I didn't get up or something. It was a bit unusual, but I didn't make too much of it. It was just nice to have her with me. The curtain was pulled around my bed because it was time for morning baths. I was asked if I felt strong enough to help myself, and I assured her I was. A nurse brought in a pill that I was going to start taking to try to help my heart. It was called Quinidine. I took my pill and my CCU nurse was still there. She said, "Oh, I have the time right now. I'll just stay here a few minutes and help you get started." I thought that was fine. She went and got the water. As a heart patient, I was not allowed out of bed this time for any reason. We were talking and I remember her giving me the wash cloth. I wiped my face off, handing it back to her, and she turned her back to me to rinse it out. I remember thinking what nice long hair she had when all of a sudden, I felt like . . . . . I was in a black tunnel. It seemed like a tunnel because of the sound of wind. At least, this is as close as I can explain it. I was being lifted upwards on a slight incline in what felt to me like a very comfortable tilt-back chair. It was dark, but not absolutely dark. I knew I was not blind, but that it was just dark. Suddenly, I thought, I don't have any pain, OH BOY, it doesn't hurt anywhere!! I felt peace, a wonderful glorious all-encompassing peace, no fear whatever. There are no human words to express the feeling. I had no thoughts of anything else, but how wonderful I felt.

As my nurse turned around, she told me she wondered why I had gotten so quiet and after rinsing the wash cloth and soaping it . . . she turned around again to give it to me, she immediately recognized I was in serious trouble. She began resuscitation, called for the crash cart and it was only two doors down the hall. This is the unit they use for cardiac conversion, like you see on T.V. where they shock the heart to get it started again. This they did. It seemed like only a short time that I was in that tunnel, but when I awoke I can remember smiling and being so at peace, and then the realization I was not in the same room and who, what are all those people around my bed? Oh, it's Mom, Dad, Mike and my brother and sister-in-law, Gayle. I smiled. "Gee, what are you all doing here?? Why is everyone so sad?? They looked like they had been crying. Then I realized I was back in CCU hooked up to the bottles and machines again. How did all this happen? Mom, leaning over the bed smiling, big tears, and all saying, what are you up to again? I went to sleep again, not realizing it was four hours later than when I went to sleep upstairs. They kept me drugged so I would remain quiet for a few days and I just could not wake up enough to be able to put things together, but as I got better I began to realize . . . I was dead, I was in a tunnel, and I was in pain again but I still had that peace with me. For now I know, it is a real place that Jesus has for us.

Now I ask you, how was I going to tell anyone about that tunnel, not one book had been written on this yet. It was not a subject that was discussed yet, and being a former epileptic, it wasn't going to be me that said anything, no sireee!!

They told me as they took me back to my room several days later that I had had an allergic reaction to my heart medicine and had a complete heart failure. The hospital was buzzing with what had happened, even the cleaning personnel, when they would be talking with me, would say, "Oh, you're the one!?"

I began to realize, what if an aid had taken care of me instead of my CCU nurse, she would have pulled the curtain, given me the equipment, and gone on to the next patient on her list. I had absolutely no warning, no pain, no nothing to have enabled me to call for help to my room-mate. I might have laid there until they came back to check on me. What if the machine had not already been on this floor? It would have been many more minutes before they got it to me. What if I had not been ready to meet the Lord? Amazing Grace.

It began to sink in that I had had a miracle, God had known that I was going to need the CCU nurse with me, and need that certain piece of equipment. Just coincidence, you say? I know different. My doctor knew different an the nurses said they knew the difference. They experience these unexplainable things quite often.

My little nurse would visit me once in a while and would just pat my hand and would get big tears in her eyes and not be able to talk to me. I thought maybe I had offended her in some way. After three more weeks I went home again, doing well and my heart would stay in rhythm about three months and then off it would race again and I would go in for a cardac conversion for a few days and my nurse would never fail to come in and sit on the bed and say how glad she was to see me and the big tears would run. By now I had had it converted twice and Mike said we just couldn't live this far from our families with me having all these problems and him driving one hundred miles a day to work. He said we had better sell the farm since I was having trouble keeping up with the big place and then my parents and his could be of more help.

**Walking 4-H calves old farm**

**Lee & 4-H steer**

**Center — Laurie & Lee with 1 & 2 place heifers.**

Our new house

Laurie, Peggy, Lee
Ready for church

Linda at stove before healing

Old front porch

Laurie & Lee going to barn

It was a big house!

Church across from farm

Lee, Peggy, Laurie — old farm

41

# Part II

# Soul

*The hardest part: letting my soul (mind) be changed to His.*

# VIII
# His Ways . . . Not Mine

Inside I had a knowing this was meant to be. But I sure didn't understand it. So, I threw a fit. Sell my barn, my woods, my cows! They were like family, they each knew their names and were all halter broke, and they were such quiet, peaceful creatures compared to our family life, I couldn't give them up. I argued on and on. I could still feed and water. I just needed help with the hay. Then my brain storm hit. I would agree to sell if we could take the cows and if we got "such-and-such" a price, set high enough that I knew I was safe.

While I was caught up in my own schemes, Mike was looking for a house in the Salem area where we could have enough cattle for the children to stay in 4-H but sell the rest. I still felt safe with my plans when Mike said he had found a really nice little place. I used all the excuses too far, too sick, kids need me home, choir practice, P.T.A., everything I could think of not to look at it. Now we had no "For Sale" signs on our farm and we had no realtor, but a couple just "heard" the farm was for sale and came to look at it. They said they wanted it and left to acquire financing. Things were not going the way I had planned!

Finally, I had to drive up to see it. As I drove in the driveway, a big lump came in my throat. I could hardly swallow and tears kept trying to flow. I swallowed and swallowed, trying not to cry in front of the realtor and owner. They were telling me how nice this and that was I couldn't see it. "It" was only a story and a half; it was really small. It had the ugliest pink living room I ever saw. This house could never compare to my big farm house. How could Mike ever think we would be happy in this! There was no barn at all and there were

360 apple trees and they would have to be moved out so we could have pasture for the cattle. I cried all the way home. I got more and more upset and was so sick at my stomach I had to stop the car and get out. My mind was so in a turmoil. "Oh, surely, we won't have to live there!"

Just as quickly, an acquaintance of Mike's who had a bulldozer said he would trade his work in taking out the apple trees on the property for some of our registered beef. The couple came back and said they had the financing AND the lady who owned the property agreed to the price Mike had offered her. Things moved so fast I couldn't keep up. The day after the children got out of school for summer vacation we moved to the little farm in Salem. I was still crying. Why? Why?

All my planning, all my objections were powerless to stop our move. I was smart enough to know something more powerful than my own will was at work in this situation. I began to read the Bible more, trying to find answers. And answers I would find. This move was the door God opened to work a deep work in my soul. Just as I could not see yet what work on the new house would bring, I could not see the work that had to be accomplished in me. But the house and I were going to be redone. I thought I knew God, but He knew I only knew in a small part.

Even though I was so unsettled inside, I settled my family into our new house. I cried out to God and tried to seek understanding through Him. I needed so many answers. He had healed me of epilepsy, brought me back to life from heart failure. How? Why? And how come? Why me??? Inside I felt all the changes as I was being drawn to Him. But I had no understanding. How I needed answers and someone to talk with, for Mike just thought I was crazy and told me so quite often. Communication between us was very poor.

At precisely this time, I answered the door one day and there stood two of my new neighbors, Carol and Clare. They had come to introduce themselves to me. We had a very nice visit and as they were leaving they said that there was a Bible study that met on our road. Would I like to come in September when the children went back to school? I actually leaped into the air as I said, "Yes!" By the look on their faces I knew I had overwhelmed both my new friends. I'm sure mine was not the usual answer they got when they asked someone to Bible study.

Encouraged by my response, they also invited me to Revival services they were having during the week at their church. I politely declined with a pleasant, "Thank you, but I have my own church." They had not asked me to come when my church had services, but I had refused anyway. I would later learn that this response was one of those things that God was going to change in me. Being religious I had God in a nice little box, but He would show me how much bigger He was.

September came and I could hardly wait to get to Bible study. One of the first ladies I met was Lela, a girl I had gone to high school with. That was a surprise! Then I met Carolyn. She had come in carrying an extra shoe. Everyone introduced ourselves and each told how we had met the Lord. Then, Carolyn, holding the shoe in her lap, could contain herself no longer. She was a Catholic who had gone to the same Revival services I had refused. She had a short leg and had worn built-up shoes for years. She confessed she had gone to the Revival out of curiosity. She did not believe in miracles but Jesus had done one in her life anyway. They prayed for her leg and the evidence sat in her lap. she now had on new shoes that were the same size heels and she had no limp. She was miraculously healed!

I had come to the study for answers but had not expected to get any so dramatically and swiftly. Here was a group of people who got excited when I began to tell what had happened to me. They would say, "That's wonderful, Linda. Praise the Lord!" I just kind of gave them that Ahummmmm! look. I had not yet learned to give Jesus the glory He deserved for what He was doing for me. As we studied the Bible together the ways of God became light to me. I began to realize that His power did not end with the early church for I was living proof of His power. How awesome a realization!

I had never heard of a "Pentecostal" before so the word didn't bother me one bit. I knew we celebrated Pentecost in church but I had no scriptural knowledge of its meaning. God would now begin to turn me in the direction of this knowledge. I could see that some of the ladies had a sparkle that I did not possess. They also seemed to smile a lot, and I wanted that. I knew that they loved me because of their actions. I knew they prayed and that often answers to those prayers came that very day. I also knew I did not know the Bible the way that they knew it. And one thing for sure, I was going to learn to pray so I would not be embarrassed when we prayed in the circle and my turn came.

God had heard my heart's cry and was answering in ways I could never have imagined.

# IX
# Gil, A Miracle Friend

One member of our Bible study was Gil. Gil holds a special place in my heart. She had come to America from Thailand after the Vietnam war with her American husband. Gil did not talk much, for she felt she could not speak fluent English. But I felt she did very well considering the fact that I could not say one word in her native tongue. Through our Bible study I was enlarging the box I had the Lord in, and I was attending some of the Wednesday night services. Since my church did not have mid-week services, I could do this. Gil would sometimes come also. One evening as the service was over, Gil asked me and Carol to pray with her. "I want Jesus in my heart," she said. She knelt at the pew, Carol on one side and me on the other. I thought my heart was going to jump out of my chest. I had never prayed with another person in all of my life. Her humility, tears and genuine love for Jesus combined to make one of the most memorable experiences I have ever known.

She shared with us that the first year of her attendance at Bible study, she could not understand the Bible at all, but that she liked everyone and her mother-in-law wanted her to come, so she came. But since she had asked the Lord into her heart, she was now able to understand what the Bible said and to read it.

With tender, child-like faith, Gil just believed what the Bible said and that was that! She began to talk to us much more and tell us things that the Lord was showing her. We did not discuss Satan or evil spirits too often because we did not have much knowledge on the subject. There is also a subtle thought in many a mind that "what I don't know won't hurt me." I found this thought a great block to my wanting to recognize

Satan and his tactics. But Gil knew many things of this nature; she began to explain them to us. She had been a Buddhist all her life, but she said inside she was always searching for something more. Gil told how she searched at shrines and temples for this peace that she longed for. One time a group of her friends left early in the morning and traveled to a big temple. In her broken English she shared, "At temple, large Buddah, we climb, we climb, we pray, we need water, we climb, get tired, get hot, climb and pray, search for Buddah to give us great blessing, climb, after 1500 steps we reach summit. No great blessing, no more peace than before, pray some more, then must leave and climb down, down same steps took all day to go up." Gil said all she received from that all day search was tiredness. But in her heart she kept on searching. She told us of watching the priests burn themselves and watching them cast spells on people and even seeing those people die. She and family and friends stayed away from the priests as much as possible. They were very afraid of them and the power they used. Gil told us of how one could feel evil move in her country. She did not like to talk too much about this because she was a little fearful even yet of the things she had witnessed with her own eyes. She did not offer information unless we asked, and even then it was hard for her to talk too much. We knew, though, by her reactions, she knew of what she spoke..

Before actually coming, Gil had felt for some time that she was going to come to America to live. When she met her husband and came to America, she said that she knew something higher in power directed it. Now she knows that it was God. The Bible says God searches the heart and Gil's heart was desperately searching for Him.

Gil and her mother-in-law became very close. She was always asking Gil to give up Buddah and believe in Jesus. Gil went to church with her out of love and the respect that oriental peoples have for their parents, but Gil did not understand church. When her mother-in-law died, Gil felt such a great loss and sorrow. In her heart, she searched to know if she would ever see her again. One night she had an experience that had our Bible study sitting on the edge of our chairs as she told us.

She awoke one night having much turmoil inside about where her mother-in-law was and was quietly crying when she felt a soothing hand rest on her head. She said it did not scare her at all. She reached up her hand and put it on top of the hand on her forehead. Gil said, "It man's hand, big, strong, rough, not want it to go away. It so peaceful, not want to turn head for it to go away, turn eyes to floor, Oh, thinking, sandles on feet, white robe, what this?" Then she slept. On waking the next morning, inside she said she knew her dearly loved mother-in-law was all right.

Gil did not know the Lord at this time or even know the Bible. She did not know how people in the Bible dressed or anything about Angels, for her only teaching had been Buddhism. After Gil had asked Jesus into her heart and shared this experience as she became freer to talk to us, she said, "You know, I think it was the Lord." We all agreed with her.

Everyone in our study was learning together. We believed in deliverances, but no one knew much about them. We would pray for the needs presented to the group. Sometimes as we stood in a circle Gil would just fall down and be engulfed in a deep peace and then get up laughing and beaming with joy. We began asking what the Lord was doing. One of our ladies said finally, "Do you think the Lord is delivering Gil from Buddhism?" As the words were spoken, we all realized we were and had been watching a sovereign work of the Holy Spirit in our midst. Gil was finally able to put away her statues and some of the mementoes that she treasured from Thailand because she realized that they were not of the God she now served. Gil was familiar with spirits and when she began to understand that there was a Spirit of God and He was called the Holy Spirit, she was able to totally receive Him in His fullness. To her, things in the Spirit world were very natural. She would come to Bible study and say, "Oh, I wake up and angel standing at bed, watching me. Oh, I smile at him and go to sleep." This was the most beautiful, open faith I had ever seen.

She began to write and witness to her family in Thailand. One day she came to study absolutely jumping up and down. She could not wait one minute to tell us of a vision she had. Gil was standing on a table in the middle of a large room; she did not know where the room was, but she thought it was Thailand, or somewhere that her people were. The people were seated in long rows like at a banquet, but there was no food on the tables. She said, "Jesus, please let me tell them about

You." And she began to tell them and she could not believe the words were coming from her. She looked at us with big tears in her eyes and said, "I want to tell them so bad what I find. I think I get to go home to tell them." Again, we all agreed with her.

Gil and her husband had one son and wanted another child, so Gil began to pray and soon she was pregnant. Toward the end of her pregnancy she was not feeling well. She was a little concerned. As always at Bible study, we never knew what God would do or show us. This time Gil had awakened and there was an angel standing near her bed. Gil said, "He reach down and touch stomach and say baby all right. It is girl." A few weeks later a beautiful baby girl was delivered to Gil and her husband, all well and healthy.

Gil has made one trip to her homeland and witnessed to her family. Now she is home and the Lord is sending people to her by way of the "Boat People" who have been adopted into this country. Gil opens her home to the families that locally have brought them here and cooks them a Thai dinner and loves them with the love she has found in Christ.

I feel honored to know Gil. The Bible says, "If ye believe," and this is what she is all about. I grew in faith as I saw her faith so simply lived. She just believed God was all that He said He was.

What was the Lord going to show me next?

# X
# The Holy Ghost Is WHAT?

In Bible study every once in a while someone would mention the "Baptism" or "heavenly language" or "power" in prayer that we needed. I had never heard anything about these experiences. I did read in my Bible about Pentecost, but I did not want to seem dumb in front of my friends, so I basically listened and watched a lot. I read some books on the subject, as my analytical mind told me to do. In my heart I knew for sure that I needed to know my God better than I knew Him. I also saw in the ladies a power and an awareness of what the Holy Spirit was doing that I did not have. I was not even too sure that I liked the term Holy Ghost. Ghost — just what did that mean? But my heart longed to know God and His Son better. If I had to call it the Holy Ghost, then I would.

I began to study and found out that the Holy Ghost was not an it, that He was a part of God, just like Jesus was. I read that Jesus said that He was going to ask the Father and that the Father was going to give me another Helper that would be with me forever and that He (Holy Ghost) was the Spirit of Truth, whom the world cannot receive because it does not know Him. Wow! That was me. I didn't know Him or of Him, so how could I receive Him? I read all that in John 14:16-31. I was given the book, *Two Sides of a Coin*, by Francis and Charles Hunter, to read. One beautiful, warm, autumn day, no one was home, so I became deeply involved with the book and was totally unprepared for the presence of God that came into the room so strongly that I was literally overcome and began to weep. I was overcome with His love for me and felt so small in His presence and just asked Him to show me what He would have me to do. I didn't understand His Holy Spirit but I really wanted to.

I felt lifted up out of my chair and three words came out of my mouth that I did not recognize. His presence was so strong and I heard Him speak to me (whether it was an audible voice or not, it was real. It was loud and I knew who He was talking to.) He said, "Daughter, now don't you ever put me in a box again, for you know different now, don't you?" I could hardly get the word "yes" out of my mouth because of that big lump in my throat and I was trembling so hard, not with fear like "scared," but fear in the sense of being in the presence of grand power. Respect is a better word. Then He said, "Whatever you think of, I am always bigger."

As I was thinking over these words, I heard a voice call, "Linda." It startled me. I did not hear a car drive in and I was a little upset to have to leave this first time experience of His powerful presence. I ran to the door. No one was there. Good, I thought. I came back to my chair, had just sat down, when "Linda." Again, it was someone calling me. I went to the door. No one there. I walked outside and out to the barn. No cars. No one in sight. Again, I returned to the room and as I sat down, very clearly the voice said, "Linda." I started to get up from my chair a little agitated this time, when I stopped and in a whisper said, "Is that You . . . Lord?" I had realized that the voice came from within me.

He spoke, "You can trust me with your very heart beat, never fear, never think too small."

One day not long after, I was so impressed to read I Samuel and in Chapter Three, I was astonished to read the Lord's call to Samuel.

Could I dare to believe that God would speak to ME like He did to Samuel? ME with all the hang-ups and problems and failures towards Him? As I pondered these things once again I was reminded, He didn't live out there somewhere. He was with me and indeed He would and will speak to anyone who is willing to hear.

You know, I sometimes doubted those three little words that were not English, but I could not doubt the way in which the Lord spoke to me and the confirmation that I read in the Bible. Since there was no way to separate the two, I had to accept it all. I felt humble, even a little bit fearful of this God who was willing to become so real in my life.

I think I better tell everyone about this so that they can know . . . I'll start on Mike!! Then Lee, Laurie, and Peggy, then . . . Dad and Mom . . . then anyone I meet at the grocery store . . . then . . .

# XI
# Testing and Trial Produce JOY

I really wanted everyone to get in on this beautiful experience, especially my husband. I tried every little "wifie" trick I knew to get him to church. I became over zealous in this. He was not having any of it. In this was a hard lesson I had to learn. Not everybody wanted to love Jesus. The Lord changes even our countenance when He lives inside of us and even more so when the Holy Spirit had given us His power. My husband had trouble even looking at me. I grinned a lot; I just couldn't help it and for some reason only the Lord knew, He just kept enlarging this Joy inside of me.

My husband's temper became more violent and our son was now old enough to step in and try to protect his mother. I in turn got very angry at Mike for the things he said to put us down. Our children were put in a situation of terrible tension and were having a rough time of it.

When he would start to rave, everyone of us would take off for different parts of the house, barn or woods. I would scream back at him out of pure frustration, which was not a great witness to my experience in Christ. I knew where his help was, but he just would not yield to the Lord.

The old saying that we hurt the ones we love most has much truth in it, but it could also be said we hurt the ones that love us the most, because the children and I loved Mike. We were easily hurt by his attacks.

Because of this terrific tension and the trouble that I already had in my joints, I would have days of terrific pain and swelling. Sometimes my neck on one side would be twice the size as the other, or my arm would swell. My knees got so large with swelling that I would not be able to use them. I would sometimes scream with pain. I would go to my bed and cry, so in torture that the only thing I could do would be to say, "Jesus, Jesus," and my few words of that spiritual language I had received. As my cry got more desperate my language became more full. I hurt so badly, I couldn't even think in English sometimes. I cried over and over, "Lord, I believe in healing! I believe! How can I not believe! Help me! Help, Help!" "The pain, Oh, God, I can't bear this joint pain. There is no place of comfort to even touch this arm. Please, Lord, let Mike come home from work and offer me some comfort." But it never happened. And so this kind of pain drove me to begin to praise the Lord. It was through clenched teeth at first but as I began to say, "Thank you, Lord, for my not being an epileptic, thank you for this beautiful family. Thank you, Lord, even though I feel like I am alone, You have proven to me that the Holy Spirit, the Comforter is always with me. John 16:6-7)

You may be thinking that I talked myself out of the pain, but I tell you if you have ever had this arthritic pain, you know you cannot talk yourself out of it. Mike would make such fun of me, "Thanking the Lord, Ha!" he would say. "You are crazy, flipped out, you don't even have anything wrong with you. If you did, it could not come and go like that." I would begin to cry, then he would get angry. I would withdraw. What a circle! What a mess. When the arthritis would hit again I would try to fight it, just so Mike would not make fun of me. "Where's your God?" Then the attack upon my mind would come. It was never from within; it was from the one whom I loved. How I have fought feeling sorry for myself, as I did fight this, JOY would begin to well up inside. I did not understand that Joy.

The tension was making this condition twice as bad. I was also scared because inside I sometimes felt that I hated this man. I knew I did not and I could not and I would not, no matter what. I thought to die would be better, but then I thought of the children. Oh, those beautiful children! No, dying was not the answer. I would sit or lie on my bed and sing the Joy of the Lord is my strength over and over until His peace settled over me, and through it would be the Joy that flows from the Spirit, it does not depend on our circumstances. It is not the same as natural happiness. It was beyond that and beyond me. I loved it. Jesus says that if we love Him, we will rejoice. John 14:28. I love Jesus, so it is my responsibility to serve the Lord with joy and gladness and because I do, then He begins to give a supernatural kind of Joy, a joy that is healing to our spirits and souls and also to our physical bodies. Proverbs 4:20-22. Remember to rejoice in what your Savior has delivered you from and then remember to rejoice in what we are being delivered into . . .

Many days I would have to call one of my good friends in the Lord to pray for me to help me get through this hour. Then sometimes the Lord would send "Sunny," my special friend from Bible study, to pray for me before I even called her. In her the Lord gave me a very close spiritual sister that felt my hurt many, many times. As her name says, she was sunshine in a storm.

I finally was persuaded to go to a healing service. Up until this time, I had resisted my friends' urgings to go to Sunday services other than at my own church. I was unknowingly affected by a religious spirit. But I needed Christ in whatever form or name was on the door.

I could not persuade my husband to go with me, but I was determined to get to this service. As I dressed and got ready I began to get excited, even got butterflies. I could not seem to get there fast enough. I knew something exciting was going to happen, but I had no idea what. The Lord would be there. That I knew . . .

# XII
# Satan??
# The Guy With Horns And A Tail?

It was January 1, 1974. There I sat in a pew about half way to the front of the church, my friends sitting on either side of me (I think to keep me from running out. That's how I felt, anyway.). The service began with much singing, and most of the songs I did not know. People were raising their hands, some were clapping their hands, singing loudly. Some would pray their own prayers while the minister was praying his prayer, and some people were "Amening" him. My first thought was, my, how irreverent they are of the minister. Then, this is okay for them, but it's too noisy for me. I cannot even think to pray in all this noise. Oh, how little I knew. The words came to me, "No BOXES," so I tried to enjoy; but I did not do too well.

When the evangelist began to preach, I had never seen anything quite like this in my church either. He walked back and forth and did not even read from any notes. Then, my, oh, my, he was reciting Scripture after Scripture, Luke 4:38-40 . . . "And they had make request of Him on her behalf. And standing over her, He rebuked the fever and it left her; .. . .all who had any sick with various diseases brought them to Him; and laying His hands on every one of them, He was healing them." Matthew 4:23, "And Jesus was going about in all Galilee, teaching in their synagogues, and proclaiming the gospel of the kingdom, and healing every kind of disease and every kind of sickness among the people." Luke 6:8-11, where Jesus told the man with the withered hand to come forward and after looking around at them all, He said to him, "stretch out your hand!" And he did so and his hand was restored. Of course, I was trying to look them up to be sure he was right, but I soon gave up. I just couldn't keep up with him. I began to like what he was saying. I began to receive the word in my spirit, not in my head. He was telling us about healing, how God wanted us to be well and how old Satan was the one who wanted to kill us and to make us sick. This was still new to me; I did n ot like to talk about the devil and his little army. As he went further in helping us to understand, I began to get very, very warm, so warm that sweat began to trickle down my face and glasses and then down my back. My clothing was getting damp. My thoughts were, "Oh, dear God, here I am in the middle of this row and I'm getting sick, and how will I ever get out without making a big commotion." Then I noticed the heat was more intense at my ankles, knees and wrists. I looked at my wrists and they were pink, and my knees were the same way. I thought I would sit very still in my pew and maybe I would not get sick. Then I began to crack. Now I was sitting as still as I could and still I was cracking. So, I thought, I'd breathe slowly and deeply, thinking this would help. I could tell people around me could hear and knew something was going on because they kept trying not to look at me. I then decided that this was enough of this silliness and I would concentrate on what the evangelist was saying. He said, "You know, people, I am finding a new thing happening in these services. God's Spirit is taking the Word and making it alive and He is not waiting for the laying on of hands at the end of a service. He just sends forth His Word and heals people right in their seats." I knew that was for me. My joints were becoming loose and the pain and stiffness was going. He said, "I love it when the Lord does things this way because then He gets all the glory."

All of a sudden I was free from that arthritis, but just as suddenly I was loosed on the inside to shout Praise the Lord! This quiet Methodist shouted her first out loud Hallelujah before I was worried about it being too noisy and irreverent. I dashed to the altar, one of the first ones down front to testify. I was healed, and as wonderful as that was the freedom to Praise the Lord, no matter who was around was greater. I was beginning to find out that tongues was not the end of the Baptism in the Holy Spirit, but just one step into a walk with the Holy Spirit in new power. Now I was released into Praise! What a wonderful night! When God said, "no more boxes," He was not kidding.

Mike was not having any of this "Full Gospel Stuff," as he called it, so we did not discuss it much. But I could not keep anything so wonderful as this from him. The kids and I came home from church that night so excited. How can you help but be excited when God has just removed the possibility of you ending up a cripple the rest of your life! We were a little late getting home because many people were hugging and kissing, they were so happy for me. The kids went into the house first. I don't know whether they told their father or not, but he was furious at our being late. He took one look at my face, and told me if I dared to say one word — just one. So I didn't. But I could not hide the glow from the touch of Jesus. I could not keep from smiling. Mike kept saying, "I don't want to hear it, all this stuff is coincidence." I hadn't said a word. He just stomped off to bed. I never did get to tell him what happened that night.

But I did get to share at Bible study and prayer meeting. Some of the ladies went to a church that did not believe that God healed supernaturally today. I thought everyone would be thrilled because they had seen me suffer with this stuff. Yet I soon learned that even people who knew Jesus personally and those who called themselves after Him, could not accept this healing. Why then did I think Mike could? This was the last Bible study these ladies attended for a long time. I felt sorry that I had offended them, but then I was so grateful to the Lord that I did not have arthritis anymore. I am sure I was a little hard to take.

Lori, one of my sisters in the Lord, said to me one day at study, "Linda, with this kind of healing you had better learn how to scripturally fight the devil." I kind of smiled at her and said, "Sure, sure. The devil, hmmmmmm!" This was all right for Gil and her country, but now, really, I'm a very intelligent person, and we don't quite believe all this way in my church. I smiled some more at her, but she had determined to tell me, so I listened. All I needed to know was that I could rebuke Satan in the name of Jesus and that God had placed His Son's name above all others. She said, "Just mean it." And she shook her finger and said, "In the name of Jesus, I rebuke you, Satan!"

Well-l-l-l, I was nice and didn't say any more. For six weeks everything went along fine. I had no pain, no swelling and I was very grateful to the Lord. Oh, was I ever thankful! I had to break the ice on the cattle's water trough because it was frozen solid. I carried twenty-four buckets of water by hand from the barn outside and my arm didn't even pinch me. I laughed and sang and acted quite fanatical, but I didn't care. That pain was no longer mine!

Then one morning, six to eight weeks later, I awoke to severe pain, as I tried to move my legs. The pain was so great I just groaned and threw back the blanket to look at two knees that were so swollen they were locked in position. At my groan my husband got up and said, "See, I told you it would not last," and stomped out of the room. He said, "Never mind my coffee, I'll get it. You stay in bed." I could not have gotten up anyway; my knees had such tremendous fever in them. Mike called the kids and told them to get ready for school, which at this age they were capable of doing. I could see the questions in their eyes as they went off to school. Mike left in a huff. Yet I could feel him laughing at me. This hurt almost as much as my knees.

There in bed I had one of the worst pity parties you can imagine. "Oh, God, why did you do this to me? How will Mike ever believe? And so on and so on." Those knees were about three times the normal size and the slightest movement sent me screaming with pain. They would not bend. I covered my head over with the blanket and cried. I had slipped back into my old way of thinking. Then I remembered what that sister said to me about the devil. It was like typing across my mind — "Rebuke Satan" — and I could see Lori shake her finger. I thought, "Well-l-l-l, I might as well try it. I couldn't hurt any more than I already did." I sat up in bed and shook my finger at my knees and said, "arthritis, in the name of Jesus, I rebuke you." At that my window cracked as if a huge stone had been thrown in. I ducked down, fearing a burglar was trying to get in. We had been having some of the local farms burglarized, and I peeked up to look over the end of our antique bed which had a very high head board and foot board, peeking slowly over it. My heart was about to jump into my throat, and I tried to see who it was. Slowly, slowly, maybe they would not see me. If they were there, I would have to get out of bed on the other side because I was in bare feet and would get that broken glass in them from the window. I looked carefully over the end of the bed and I could not believe my eyes. The window was perfect, not even a crack. I jumped up and went to look out, pulled the curtain back, and then realized, "I'm up!" I looked at my knees, fever gone, pain gone, swelling gone!! Then I knew that I would never again doubt the existence of Satan or belittle the lying power he had. No longer would I be liable to be deceived because of ignorance. I was going to listen to the Lord's Words to His disciples when He said, "Take heed . . . be not deceived." But I knew I did not want to be any closer to Satan than I was on that morning.

I asked the Lord to forgive me that I had thought He had done this to me. What a lesson I was learning about fighting real disease or symptoms that seemed just as real.

That evening Mike came home from work and said, "Oh, I see you are up, huh?" I said, "Yes," and smiled. He asked who had been messing around at the bedroom window? My mouth dropped open; I went to look outside. There was snow on the ground. We had a circle drive that went around the back of the house and just below the window was a jumble of footprints that went out from the window and on to where the drive had been plowed and were gone. They were large, but they looked human. I just stood there with my mouth open. Chills were running up and down my neck and my hair felt as though it were standing up. Mike said again, "What was going on?" The only thing I could think of was to say, "Oh, I guess the children were walking backwards in the snow." I was surprised when he said, "O.K." The children had been at school all day and none had feet as big as those prints were. Mike was thinking I had a visitor but I was not going to tell him what kind I did have. There is no way he would have believed it.

I have been free from the arthritis for quite a number of years now. Yet I have had to battle the symptoms for they have tried to reattach themselves to me especially when I would go to share my testimony at different churches or Aglows. I began to study in Matt. 4 what Jesus did when He was being tempted. He said, "It is written," and used what His Father said. In verse 11, Satan left Him. So as I was learning to walk in this new area of healing I began to say the same things if Satan tempted me with the old symtoms. "It is written by His stripes I am healed" or whatever Scripture the Holy Spirit brought to me that the Father had said. I knew I could not make a doctrine out of this, for no boxes were ever present with me, but at this point in my life this was the path I was on. I knew the name of Jesus was above every other name and now I was learning in the beginning was the Word and that Word was Jesus. So as I learned to use the Word (Jesus), He gave to me, it was still Jesus who was overcoming for me.

I had a great need to seek for the truth in all these experiences so I could be very clear in sharing what was truly happening. That I might be totally free from Satan's lies and his deceptions, also my assumptions and the false neutrality of saying, "Well, I just don't know."

So I began to walk toward learning God's laws and conditions upon which He works.

# XIII

# Presumption

My children and I began to attend a Full Gospel church because I felt I needed more answers and the people in my church did not understand "my testimony," nor have answers for me. You will notice I said, "my testimony." This was to be the next lesson for me.

I was still having times of arrhythmia of my heart when a new group of ladies came into our Bible study who were into "positive confession" very heavily. That familiar still small voice cautioned me and yet everything that was said sounded so good to me and after all the Lord had done for me, I surely could believe that I was healed in the name of Jesus. I was told that if you have faith enough you can just throw away your pills and you will be all right and that is just what I did. I kept saying, "by His stripes I am healed," and this worked in fighting the symptoms of arthritis, so I began to confess that my heart was healed. I didn't have to take pills because I was healed.

One service at church a brother came up to me with resentment and said, "The Bible says God has no favorites, but with you I don't believe it!" His words hit hard. I covered the impact by saying, "Well, if you can't handle it, I'm sorry, but you are not going to put condemnation on me, brother." I felt very justified in saying this to him.

But then came the questions. Why did the Lord seem to do all these things for me? Why, did I make my brother in the Lord feel like this about me? Was this all in my being somebody special?

No! I knew within me I really was no more special than any others. Why would God heal me of epilepsy when I did not even believe that God did these things? Why would He save my life after the heart surgery? Deep in my heart I heard the words, "Great Grandma Emma." I thought this strange. I didn't even know much about her, so I asked my mother about Great-Grandma. Mother said, "You know, they used to call your Great-Grandmother a fanatic. She attended all the church meetings she could get to. I've got her old Bible here someplace. I'll give it to you. Linda, this is the fifth or sixth Bible she wore out reading. She read her Bible a lot."

In the pages of that old Bible, I found a most wonderful letter that Emma had received from her brother. The letter talked about our salvation and how we had to let Jesus be Lord of our lives, about how ill he was feeling, but that he knew the angels were waiting to greet him and how he would be waiting to see her when she got to heaven. Her letters and notes talked the same way. Lights began to go on in my head and then when I found the clippings in her Bible about receiving the baptism of the Holy Spirit, I asked the Lord what He was showing me? You know, the Lord very rarely speaks directly to us. It is with impressions, thoughts dropped into our minds, that very small voice we can easily miss, that still small voice seemed to say, "Daughter, you are blessed by a great grandmother who prayed prayers of faith for you before you were even born. Prayers of faith never die because I remember them always." I was overwhelmed. It was not me, but Great-Grandma Emma Jane (after whom I am named) and God in His faithfulness who were so special. Genesis 18:19. Mother said she always sat in the Amen Corner. I didn't know we had one. Grandma was absolutely sure of her salvation and her white dress. Why hadn't someone helped me be that sure? Grandma knew her obedience to the Lord would be rewarded, that obedience was better than sacrifice. Why had not someone taught that to me all my years in church? But again because of the supernatural work of the Holy Spirit within me and His faithfulness to lead me to all truths (as the Bible says He will), I knew I had to forgive myself and my former church so I could walk in peace.

Then one night in choir practice at our new church my heart began to slow down. I felt I was just slipping away and I laid my head over on my friend Peg's shoulder and said, "I feel funny." They could not get a pulse. I gave them quite a scare and they began to pray and pray. As they prayed, I began to feel stronger, and was completely okay by the evening service.

But my "confessed healing" was not there. Another evening service, contrary to the last experience, my heart started to race. I could hardly breathe; my heart was so tight. After service the pastor and a few friends anointed me with oil and everyone who had their hands on me felt my heart give a jolt. It went back into rhythm. We all left praising the Lord.

The next morning I awoke and I knew I was in serious trouble. I did not say anything to Mike because he just did not want to understand and I was tired of being belittled. My breathing was very shallow and my color was completely gray. I was drenched in a cold, clammy sweat. If Mike had looked at me, he could not have helped but to see, but such was the condition of our marriage. I was crying, "Oh, Lord, I testified that I was healed, my heart went into time. What is happening? What is Mike going to think? What is everyone at church going to think?" There was a tremendous spiritual battle going on and I was so young in this area that I did not perceive it fully. The prince of death watches our lives and he would steal any of our lives easily if we enabled him to do so, and I came so close. Frustrated, confused, crying, I went to bed, just felt like I would like to die. I was ready to quit. I shut the curtains, sat on the bed because I could not breathe had I lain down. I just intended to give up. There was a knock at my door. I had forgotten this was the day of Bible study and the gals were coming to pick me up. They knew I was there and they knocked at the doors and windows and called me and called me. Finally, I looked out the window and just waved them on. Just go on!

Lori took one look at my face and knew I was in real trouble, but I wouldn't let anyone in. They went on to study and began to pray unceasingly for my life. They also called the pastor to let him know how I looked. He and one of the deacons and his wife jumped into their car and started to my home.

In the meantime I was telling the Lord that I was done. Just leave me alone! This time He talked back to me, and said, "Is that really the way you want it, Linda?" Stubbornly, I said, "Yes." He said, "O.K." For the briefest moment, I felt Him withdraw. I was never so terrified in my life. I never felt such blackness or fear like it. In the quickness of a blink of the eye, I realized what I had done and screamed, "Oh, Lord, I'm sorry.

Please, I didn't mean what I said! I'll just follow you as best I can." At that moment, my pastor and friends arrived. I let them in and they sat me down and laid hands on me and they prayed and rebuked and praised and still I was very ill, very wet with perspiration. Finally, the pastor said to me, "We are not going to be foolish. I don't understand all this either, but you are going to the hospitall."

I called my husband and he came home and took me back to Akron. I was to be cardioverted again, but coming and going in my thoughts was the word balance — find the balance.

I was put in a room with a lady who was experiencing deterioration of her spine, and I was put on my medication again. Along with that serious condition she happened to be a Spirit-filled Christian. Deloris and I studied the Word together much of the day. I watched her as the pain would come. She had had so many shots that she had scar tissue in all the normal places that one would receive a shot. They were having to give her pain shots in the stomach and even that was so tough they had to punch her to inject her. I would watch Deloris as she began to praise the Lord when she could not take any more pain, and it seemed the Spirit of the Lord would take her away somewhere, where I could not get to. She would be talking, praising the Lord and singing. I would talk to her and she never heard me. Then when she came back she was able to tolerate the pain. I was ever so confused, but I watched. As we would be talking about things in the Word, she would say, always find the balance. She would just mention how hungry she was for a few dill pickles. In a few minutes an orderly would show up and say, "I was just thinking about you and thought you might like a snack, so I brought you some dill pickles." She would just be so loving and kind and witnessed to everyone who came in, mostly by her actions, not words. Another time she said, "Oh, for a lettuce and tomatoe!" The nurse appeared at the door saying, "This came up from the kitchen and I thought of you and wondered if you might like them?" What else — a plate of lettuce and tomatoes! I had never, never seen anything like this. She began to tell me about suffering and positive confession and again repeated that one should find the balance. My mind was beginning to settle down.

The day I was to go down to ICU for the cardioversion, the

nurse who had helped in saving my life after heart failure came in to visit me and Deloris. She discussed what had happened to me and this little nurse told me that she had been a Christian for quite awhile. The day of the heart failure she felt so strongly to go with me to the floor that she had taken her break to be with me and to help me with my bath. She said that she had never realized that these urges were the Lord talking to her, and that was the day she knew that the Lord had put her there in that place and time to be used to save my life. That is what all her tears were about when she would sit with me on the bed. What a neat thing for Jesus to do, to explain what He had done. And to top it off, I noticed a real difference in my doctor. I learned that he had become born again. Now, not only was he a great doctor, but he was on the staff of the Great Physician. I was rejoicing! In the midst of what looked like a terrible circumstance, I came out rejoicing!

I meditated on all that was happening. I began to ask the Lord what He would have me to know. He began by reassuring me that the day I told Him to leave, He was there by me all the time, but that I had to be shown what I asked for was very dangerous. That is one mistake I will not make again! Then the Lord impressed me with the Scripture, Phil. 1:6; I had no idea what it was, but when I looked it up, I knew that whatever happened, I would have the Word: *"Being confident of this very thing, that he which hath begun a good work in you will perform it until the day of Jesus Christ."* I was going to have to literally stand on this Scripture in the days to come, but I knew that God had given it to me. I had not picked it out for myself. I was determined I would not so easily give in to sickness as my friend, but I would also not take on a position of presumption either.

When I went back home and then back to church, a lot of people were watching me. A couple of sisters said, "Well, now, there must be some terrible sin in your life or this would not have happened." The props went out from under me again. First I had been accused of being a favorite and now accused of being sinful. I grabbed onto my verse. The Lord began to minister to me about not taking these things into myself, just leaving it in His hands. This was hard, I kept saying, "Lord, what is the matter with me? I seem to offend whether I go forward or backward. Please help me."

Again I heard Him speak in the same voice I heard the day I had been baptized with the Holy Spirit. He said, "Daughter, after all we have been through, can you trust Me?" "Yes, Lord." "Really trust me even if it seems different from what others keep trying to tell you?" "Yes, Lord." Then he said, "I will never leave you, but be watchful of what you say, nor will I give you more than I know you can take. Still trust me." By this time in my life when the Lord asked me three times I knew that new things were coming my way. I was learning not to question Him so much and just go on believing in His goodness toward me.

The Lord seemed to say a most wonderful thing. I has meant life and peace to my soul and body. I seemed to hear, "Linda, do you want me to heal you right now, because you know and believe I can, so you can be satisfied and not be embarrassed any more? Or do you really trust Me and will let Me by the choice of your own will decide when it is the right time so I will get the glory that is due Me?" What a question! What could I say? I just want to be of help to people. I have something inside that wants to help, was my prayer. (Of course, that something was placed there by my original call to be a missionary.) With this, the Lord flooded my heart with a new hope and love and a confident understanding of the healing of my heart. You see, I might not know all the places of Scripture by heart, nor can I quote them chapter and verse to perfection, and if you can, God bless you. but in my heart that day I knew and still know that my God loves me. He wants me to be well and He does not want me to be in pain any more than my earthly parents would want me to suffer and I cannot presume to tell Him how I expect Him to move, when and where. He is God, not me. Above all else, I want to be in His will and I am trying to get the self of Linda to die and the spirit within her to grow. "Do whatever, Lord."

In a few months I had become allergic to that heart medication and the doctor took me off. I did not have to do it myself.

The Lord showed me my reaction to that dear brother, that thought I was God's favorite, was a reaction to the truth of God exposing pride. Then I found out that the man had been praying for a healing of his heart for many years. I could now begin to truly love those people who accused me of sin because my pride was being broken and I knew the Lord would deal with my sins. I was being freed to love His people. I did not have to be anyone special or prove anything.. I was beginning to know who I was in Christ and that we are all a special people to Him. But yet, with His sovereign hand He chose to touch my life and perform miracles in me and through me. And I had to learn not to taint His sovereign work with my pride.

He had brought me down to lift me up in Him.

Hallelujah! I was becoming a new creation. I was learning to live from my spirit, not my mind (soul). This process was where I would next walk with the Lord. And in His loving way He always gives us something that causes us to stretch out toward Him if we desire to.

I had a vision. I was fully aware I was sitting in my church pew, and yet I was not. I was not asleep, for I was aware of seeing something that was not the front of my church, yet I was still aware of being in church. For just a moment, I had a small shiver of fear, as a former epileptic the thought and moment of doubt was there. I had to remember that if there was a false sense of being in the spirit, then there was the real, for there cannot be a negative without the positive. So I whispered, "Jesus," as I was placed on a small crevice in the side of a rocky mountain. I was hunched down with my arms wrapped around my legs. There were great shadows on the rocks and as they moved I thought the sun was coming up, but the light came closer around the side of the path that went around the rock where I was. A voice said, "Don't look," and a shadow covered my small crevice for a slight moment and then the light had gone on past me and the voice said, "I will be with you." I answered, "Whatever is happening here, I am not moving." I began trembling on the inside and not yet being comfortable in this depth of spirit my soul-power (mind) thought, "Linda, you have had too much Cecil D. DeMille. I was seeing and experiencing this, but also knew there was a church service still going on around me. I have learned that this is called a vision and it is different than a dream. The Lord, knowing that I needed further revelation so that I could not put this experience down to what I could imagine, took me immediately to the steps of what I thought must be the steps up to the temple. There I was about three deep in a huge crowd of loud people. I could not understand what they were saying. There was so much commotion, everyone trying to talk at once. Pushing and shoving and crying and pointing up the steps. I pushed my way toward the front so I could see what they were pointing at. There, at the top of the stairs, a once beautiful curtain with gold woven through it was hanging in the doorway, ripped and shredded and now I could understand some of the hysteria as they were saying, "I was just standing here and rip it went! It got so dark in the sky!" I was now in the front row of the crowd. A priest was coming up the steps. My thought was "High Priest," as he came closer and closer, he stopped in front of me and looked directly into my eyes and then I became him, or he became me, or whatever — I was now the one walking up the steps from then on. As I reached the flat part at the top of the stairs, I walked directly through the ripped curtain into a room that was alive with smoke. Smoke that was there, but not there, it did not hang there, it moved. It did not smell like any smoke I knew . . . That was it. I was back in the service, shaking from the power that I felt, trickles of tears coming from the corners of my eyes, awestruck, knowing that it was God, but what would I do with this? This was so close to the counterfeit in those seizures that I used to experience of being some place before, but I knew the counterfeit left me banging my head, biting my tongue. This left me knowing it was God and a peace. Knowing that during the entire episode I was in control and could stop it anytime that I wished. The counterfeit took away my control. There can be more to epilepsy than just the physical.

Such a little house

Ugly pink living room

Its transformation

Lee, Peg, Laurie walking calves

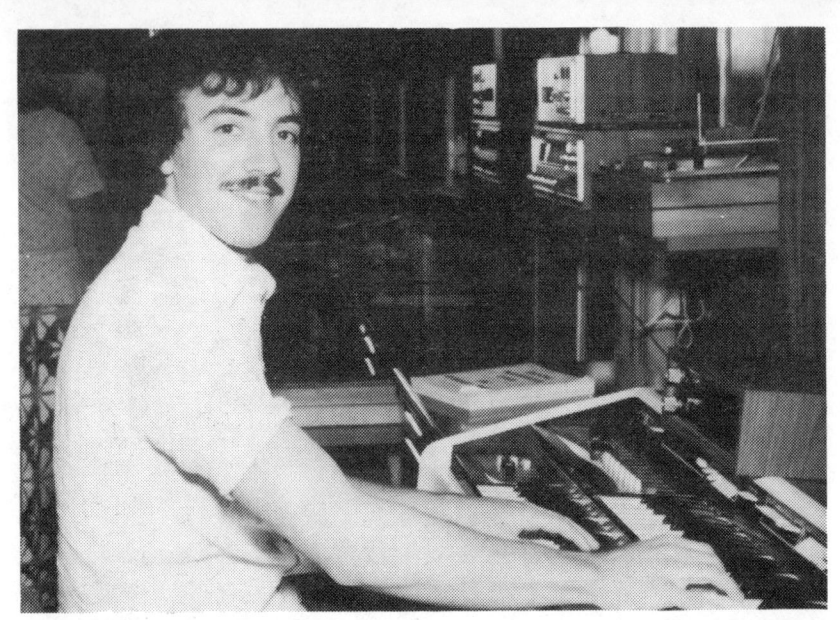

**Lee & his organ**

**Great-grandparents, Joe & Emma Fitzpatrick**

**Peg & Laurie**

# Part III

# Spirit

*Learning the difference between soul and spirit.*

# XIV
# Learning Obedience

You know sometimes you think your heart will burst if you cannot get closer to the Lord. This knowing that the Lord wants to show you something is consuming and it is so difficult to keep everything in order when you have your family to minister to also.

A couple of gals and I were searching for more of God. We just could not be satisfied with just being saved. We wanted to grow deeper into this experience of being baptized in the Holy Spirit. We knew the drawing of the Holy Spirit to prayer and needed to know exactly what this was and what God would have us to do. So we met whenever we could to pray and wait on the Lord for directions.

We studied the word and prayed and the Lord began to show us marvelous things in prayer and send us many answers. He also sent us people to teach us and help that hunger in our hearts.

Others began to call our little group and ask us to pray. Sometimes they would give us the prayer request and then the whole story that went with it. We did with every earnestness pray for the needs. But if something in the church was not going right, we began to discuss it and then pray for the need. In all honesty, we thought we were doing right. The youth pastor did this and said this and Mrs. so and so seems to be in trouble. What we said was true, but what we did not know was that Satan wanted to render us ineffectual by so slyly pulling us into a critical attitude. Satan's ploys are to destroy the works of God through unlearned Saints. As for me, that is just what Satan did. One of the ladies said one day, "You don't think this is gossip, do you?" We all laughed. "Why, no. How else are we going to know how to pray? After all, God doesn't always give you supernatural insight." Let me tell you, I could not get away from that statement: "Is this gossip?" It plagued me and I would put it in the back of my mind. I rebuked it and refused it and still it was there. I talked to myself, trying to calm my spirit with "I love the pastors and my teachers and the people and I want to help them," and I meant that. One day my son heard me talking on the phone, discussing a prayer problem. In his honest, open way, he said, "Mom, you sound a lot like a gossip to me." It pierced me like a knife, but my reaction was anger toward him. I said, "Son, you just don't understand about these things yet." I returned to the phone and continued to tell my prayer partner what Lee had said and we laughed.

When the "hound of heaven" begins to tell you something or show you, you can refuse and refuse to let truth in, but if you are truly seeking the Lord, He works and works on you. That is what finally happened and I listened and the Lord said, "You have let a critical spirit into your life and WE WILL NOT GO ONE STEP FURTHER UNTIL YOU LET ME DELIVER YOU OF THIS." I knew His voice and I knew He meant business, and I also knew that the thing I wanted to do most was to go on with Jesus.

My church did not believe you could be saved and spirit filled and have any of these kinds of spirits in your life. I was confused. Yes. But Jesus had said, "Follow me, not man." I knew the Lord had taught me about healing when I did not know anything, so I knew He could teach me about this, too.

He gave me very specific instructions and remembering what He had said about going further with Him, I listened. He impressed me that it might look like I was going to have to stand alone, but that He would always be there. I was to be quiet and let nothing negative be spoken and also I was not to say anything in defense of my stand. I really did not know what He meant by this, but I would learn.

I was to refuse this spirit of criticism. I was not to think or say anything about any of the other sisters in my prayer group and I was *not* to judge any one of them, whether this was criticism for anyone else, but me. He said, "I will deal with each one as I will and as I know their heart." This was a tall order but I started trying to do what was asked. I refused criticism and the more I refused it the more I was able to recognize it. But the part about being quiet, I was having a tougher time with. You see, being raised by my parents to do and think on my own, I was also able to speak my mind and discuss what I thought, so this was difficult for me.

In prayer group when I would try, so gently, to say something about how I was not permitted to do this any more, I would just get these looks and then the Lord would be right there, saying, "take no offense and give none. Be quiet." I would have to pull away a little. I tried to say little things, but I felt their defenses come up. I cried many a night after they withdrew from me. Then it got bad at school, for all of our children went to the same school. You know how children hear what we parents say and bring it to school and tell others their interpretations of what was said. Mine would come home with what was being said about me and the Lord would say, "Uh-uh, only positive, loving things are to come forth." I would say, "But Lord, if I could only explain about this criticism." He would answer, "My Spirit must handle it." It was hard!! The girls came home one day and said, "They said you (meaning me) are too good for your friends any more. You think the Lord is going to use you more than them." I would have to stop and say, "Father, is that the way I'm coming across?" I would answer Peggy and Laurie, "Oh, honeys, sometimes you don't hear just exactly what is said when things are repeated." I would tell them not to get mad at their friends, and to just say that the Lord was working on their Mom.

Then the Lord showed me I was living in an environment of criticism. The children and I were never given any encouragement. From cleaning to cooking, it was never right. I realized then that the children must have one positive influence to help them not let this negative spirit be a part of the family line as they grew up. This thing was bigger than just my little prayer group.

The Lord moved the group apart. One day I felt I should share and go and ask forgiveness of one of the sisters if I had offended her in any way. I shared I was involved with a critical attitude and that I was in no way including her in this. But she completely ignored me.. Once again the Lord had to remind me to take no offense upon myself and to give none. "Keep your love for her, knowing that I am working with you both."

I learned I could be critical if I wanted, I could judge if I wanted, I could get mad if I wanted, but I also learned that if I would let these things go and in obedience listen to the Word of God, I would not be disappointed. Obedience to the Lord filled me with such joy, such joy in every situation, that people continually ask where it all comes from. Obedience . . .

Obedience is the opposite of rebellion and it was helping cancel out the negative effects of the rebellion I had sown.

Your testimony:

>Is Satan trying to trap you through gossip or another means?

>Have you entertained a critical spirit or been aware of its effects?

>How has God spoken to you about obedience?

# XV
# HIS Kind Of Love

Our son to whom God had given such a gift of music so that he could hear a song one time and then sit down and play it on the organ by ear won many talent shows. He could fix just about anything mechanical. He was pleasant, giving, and hard working. Anyone who needed help knew he was there. He began suddenly to change. He wouldn't help, unless pushed. He did not like being at home, it seemed; he wouldn't talk. He was having trouble standing the criticism and abuse, the fighting and tension with his father and all that was in our home. He and his sisters had prayed so much for their dad and felt that the Lord did not care and neither did dad. So Lee decided he would just do his own thing and show us all. My, what heartache when you can see it coming, you know why it is coming and you cannot stop it. But I had given the children to the Lord and I knew I had to leave the responsibility of fatherhood with Mike. Trying to do this God's way, it was very difficult. I can stand anything, but don't touch my kids. This was something I had to leave with the Lord. Lee withdrew and did not care about anything. He was hurting.

After a couple of serious accidents and situations at school this rebellion led Lee and his father to the pastor's office where they both asked the Lord into their lives. What a marvelous thing the Lord had done. Mike began to attend church with us and we became acquainted with a nationally known evangelist who had come to our church for a week of services. Mike was baptized in water on New Year's Eve. What a difference in his speech. Mike was now managing my father's steel stamping business. The people at the shop just couldn't believe that this was the same boss they had. We were invited to go and visit this evangelist whenever she was in the area. We helped in the crusades and began traveling with her locally. We watched how God provided for us in many ways. We were even so blessed as to get to go to P.T.L. with her and get a personal tour. But Lee just watched. He wasn't sure.

Slowly some of the Christian men began to get on Mike about his smoking and some were very critical even wondering how he felt he could be saved and still smoke. This became a stumbling block and Mike soon had his eyes on the brethren who found fault, just as he was finding fault with them. My heart was breaking for Mike and for Christian brethren who judge, and I was trying to deal with my anger. God forbids our judging one another. Jesus went even further than that . He looked right at our sins and then right past them and saw the capacity of the heart and believed for the best in each. If we would look to the heart of each other we would have a lot less judgment. I could not get through to Mike that if he kept his eyes on Jesus, then he would never be disappointed; he just could not and would not see this. I was having a real problem trying not to be angry because he was using this as an excuse to fall away. I could see it and again could not stop it. The Lord reminded me about sowing and reaping, lovingly He told me how I had been forgiven, but to remember that way in the beginning of this marriage I had sown disobedience and the seeds were scattered far and it was taking many years to reap all this seed. He loved every person who was in my life just as much as He loved me and was moving in His mercy and long suffering in each person's life that had been touched by my disobedience and that I would have to trust in Him fully and let Him reap in His time, not mine, and if I could learn this, I would learn a great lesson in patience and love.

Mike was soon backslidden into this very deep criticism and became much more violent than before. Not only one spirit invaded, but it brought many more with it. The Lord impressed me that one day I would be called on to rebuke this in him. I said, "Now, hold it, Lord! I don't think I can do that." He said, "When I have prepared the way and when I say NOW, you must take the authority I have given you, for your sake." Well, I did not want to think on this too much so I pushed it back. God's presence with me makes me able to grin. I can't help it. I just grin a lot. He makes me happy! One night after church we had come home, and I really did not want to watch a particular show on T.V. so I was sitting in the other room reading. Then Mike insisted that I sit with him and watch T.V. Well, I did not argue, but I told him that I did not appreciate that language or watching such a show, so, as he watched, I read. I began to get this feeling of danger, as I looked at him, he began to get up off the couch and come towards me, saying, "You are not going to read that Holy stuff!" The Lord said, "NOW!" Before I even thought of what I was doing I rebuked Satan in the name of Jesus and it was if a balloon was let loose and Mike just sat back down on the couch and looked at me, stunned. I jumped up and went to bed.

He was very cool toward me for a long time. And I was very cool to him, which certainly was not wise, but I just did not know what to say. One day as we were discussing LOUDLY, I tried to tell him about how if we let a spirit back in that the Lord has delivered us from, the Bible says that seven more would come back with it. Maybe this was not wise either, but I felt I had to get the Word into him somehow. He got so mad that he pushed past me to go out the back door. As he left he shoved me so hard that the window sill corner punctured my back between two ribs. I felt like my back was broken and into my mind came this scripture, "Now it's unto blood, now it's unto blood." Mike came back into the house and took one look at me and said, "Oh, my goodness, what happened?" I thought, what an act — to pretend that he doesn't know. I am sure that my looks conveyed those exact feelings and more.

"Well, it's unto blood now, Mike," I said as I gathered myself up and stomped into the bathroom because I could feel the blood trickling down my back. He kept saying, "I didn't do that," but I would not speak to him.

I got my Bible out because "unto blood" sounded like King James to me. It was Hebrews 12:4: "Ye have not yet resisted unto blood, striving against sin."

Yes, that's it, Lord, now you are going to take care of this. But you know what the Lord told me to do? Ask forgiveness in my part of this. "Oh! Oh, but Lord, he did . . . he said . . . he." This time I felt Him speak to me so firmly . . . . "You ask forgiveness for your part and you must already forgive him for his part." . . . . "But Mike did not ask me to forgive, why do I ?"

I realized I was arguing with the Lord about being right. In my heart I could feel this great swelling love of Jesus for Mike and me when He said, "Linda, I was right, too, and I opened not my mouth all the way to the cross. For both of you. Linda, you have been shown much mercy and much grace, exceedingly so, so much of you is required in return."

Someone had said to me some time ago, to just put God first and everything else would be all right. I believed that and there is truth in it, but by putting God first, I thought that meant being in every church service and helping any time the church needed me. Going to as many Bible studies as I could so I could be in the Word — there is a part truth in all that. The more "Word" I learned, the more I could quote that at my husband and then I would be speaking only God's Word to him. After all, was not that a part of our armour of God — a sword — Ephesians 6:13-20. As I began to swing that sword I began to cut Mike up as I wielded that sword, no one was going to keep me from putting God first. Whack! off went an arm! Whack! off went an ear! There was my husband bleeding to death, and I smiled because I was only giving out what God said. But DID GOD SAY? What a mistake! In the first place, I was imagining this huge Crusader type sword of God and what it really meant when the Bible says sword of truth is a small type dagger, one that does not kill, but cuts like a surgeon's knife — to clean so that we can be healed, and, secondly, I was not giving out what God said for the situation. I was just giving out the Word at random. It does not work that way. The worst part and yet it shows Jesus' willingness to let us be a part of His work, although we are not perfect was: I was praying for the sick and some were recovering. I was prophesying and it was coming true. He answered prayer. Oh, that I would have known the Order in the Government of God which I have included after Chapter Seventeen. But I would learn, and God is gracious and long suffering to help us rectify our mistakes. You'll see . . .

I knew the Lord meant that all these times that I am right about so many things that if I don't temper myself with His mercy and love, my rightness becomes self-righteousness???? Oh, how I hated that revelation of myself. As the tears began to splash, I felt Him say, "I desire to rid you of this, daughter, but you must renounce having to be right all the time and then

I'll do the work." I lay crying a long time as the Lord released me.

I finally got up enough nerve to talk to Mike about it and asked him to forgive me. I thought he was going to say, "That's okay, honey. You forgive me, too," but he laughed at me and said he didn't forgive me and that I was a "such and so."

I almost fell right back into the trap again, but the Lord just wiped away the anger and said, "not a word. You know, daughter, he is so jealous of Me because of what people have told you was right in putting Me first that I cannot get through to him." I said, "Now, Lord, that is ridiculous. How can a person be jealous of God?"

"Oh, you are right again, Linda?"

I said, "No, No, No! I'm not right!" I began to see how entangled this thing could be.

"Lord, I can't love. I'm tired and I'm hurt." But the Lord never let me get away with self-pity as deep inside I could hear Him say, "If you will permit me, Linda, I can pour out my love into you. I am a creator and can create love. It will mean being willing to be hurt over and over. Taking no offense. Walking in forgiveness. Always being ready to give love and never expecting it in return. Recognize your enemy. It is not Mike, but Satan."

I would have to learn to keep my mouth shut and not fight back. It required my giving up so many of the things I thought God was first in and letting Him direct. It would require giving Him my will one more time.

He again reminded me that He would always give me opportunity to consider the cost of each step we would take. That the next few years were going to take obedience in listening to His Spirit like I had never done before. The price was going to require greater responsibility. To whom much is given, much is required. But then He always tells us the good, too, that the reward was a love for those who did not love me far beyond my being, blessings that I had not even imagined, and in obedience a peace and joy that I could hardly be able to contain. Romans 5:3-5 was being made life to me and not only this, but we also exult in our tribulations, knowing that tribulation brings about perseverance; and perseverance proven character; and proven character, hope; and hope does not disappoint, because the love of God has been poured out within our hearts through the Holy Spirit who was given us. The Lord had helped me to rid myself of self-righteousness and truth and light poured into me anew. I began to seriously listen for the Holy Spirit's directions and I could even tell when He was speaking through my husband. I knew I had committed my feet to the path and I was leaving my husband in His hands.

Your testimony:

> Are there children or loved ones you've had to learn to entrust to God?
>
> Have well meaning Christians been a stumbling block for you or others? Has your criticism of others been a stumbling block for their Christian growth? What has God shown you?
>
> Have you had to learn to keep silent and be willing to be hurt? How did you come through?
>
> Did you know that rebellion to God is compared to witchcraft in I Samuel 15:33? (KJV)
>
> How about self-righteousneess? Do you need to be right all the time?
>
> Did you know that self-righteousness is what killed Jesus?

# XVI
# It's Not An Easy Road

Things got worse at home. Some of my dear friends wondered how long I could take the tension. Out of love for me they said, "Why don't you just leave?" The hardest part was watching the abuse our children took, always being put down, being sworn at and never being able to complete a task to his satisfaction. Their grandparents on Mike's side of the family would say they would not come back to visit any more and watch the children being treated this way. No one dared to speak of this to him — not his mother, not me — for you never knew who would be the target for his anger. So we all began to make large circles around him. It was safe if there were many people around. I tried to keep many people around.

So many people wondered why I would stay in that situation with the kids. There are so many answers from very good ones, like God said, to some very sick ones, but as a Christian I can only answer for me. In me, I was trying to follow the leading of the Holy Spirit in the love of Jesus for Mike and praying that God would restore that which the cankerworm had destroyed and use all these things I had committed to Him for good.

I'll tell you how this began to work for me. We were gentleman farmers. We did not really have to work on Sunday, but, to Mike, Sunday was just another day. One Sunday we were all working here and there with grass, garden, etc., and I got a little hyper, saying, "This is Sunday. We need some rest." Of course, Mike thought I was just being lazy and began to scream. I said, "You know the pastor says that the Bible says if you don't treat your wife right that your prayers will not get answered."

The minute that this left my lips I knew I had made a

mistake. We were yelling back and forth over the noise of the tractor, but then we heard a loud BANG! The tractor that Mike was sitting on, its right front tire blew out, scaring me speechless. As I saw it sinking, I tried not to laugh at the look on Mike's face, but I couldn't help it. He was angrier than ever and then he really let me have it — BANG! The other front tire blew out and as the air hissed out of it, I was holding my side, laughing, and now Mike was speechless. I ran for the house. I did not want to say a word. Was the Lord trying to show us how silly we were being?

I was doing most of the feeding of the cows. How I enjoyed the farm work and the sweet smell of the hay. The peace I felt around the animals was a haven for me. I could talk to them, cry, or just sit in the barn and they would just blink those big brown eyes of compassion at me.

My husband's biggest complaint at this time was that the house was never clean enough to suit him. He was a white glover, but to my mind, it was not the spotlessness of a home, but the special little things that were done for one another — being a part of the school things for the children, helping the needy, seeing that the animals were taken care of — these were just as important as a spotless house. So this was one area in which I seemed to fail. In addition, my crazy heart kept going in and out of time, so I really needed help. The Lord knew and sent one of my friends to help with the housework. She needed a little extra money and I needed her. We prayed a lot and sang. The Lord had sent me a tension reliever at just the right time. And the house was much more to Mike's liking.

One thing I had always insisted on was that we all sat down to supper together and especially on Sunday noon after church. But this turned into a time of constantly being put down. One Sunday dinner I had cooked a roast beef dinner that we were enjoying. Mike got a tough piece of meat and insisted that I picked that piece out especially for him. He took his plate and dumped it down the front of me, squishing the mashed potatoes into my chest. The kids did not know whether to run or cry. I was getting angry, when in my heart I heard "take no offense." It was so loud that it startled me. I looked down at the potatoes and gravy and began to grin. It was a mess, just like Laurel and Hardy. The laughter was harder for Mike to take than the anger. But most importantly, the Lord had done something in me. Even now when I write this, it makes me laugh. It was such a mess. The plate slid from my chest, but the potatoes stayed. The gravy oozed and the peas rolled.

Your testimony:

> Have there been times when God has caused you to laugh in impossible situations?
>
> Has the Lord ever sent someone special just when you've needed them?
>
> How long were they in your life? What relationship did God produce?

# XVII
# Back To My Beginning

Selling the farm! Moving back to Washingtonville; back to my home town! Buying my family home from parents because they could no longer handle running the family business! The decision to move was quite sudden. I needed time to adjust, but got none. We were needed by my family to run the business since my father had had a stroke.

The final realization that I was being moved out of my comfortable church to the little church I was raised in came when Mike said, "Well, I'll go to church with you in Washingtonville, but not to the other one." I knew this was the Lord sending me home, but yet I still had mixed feelings and some doubts. What about the children's Sunday School training that was so good where we were? What about the freedom to fellowship in the Spirit? On the other hand, these were lovely people whom I had known since childhood, and I carried such a burden for my denomination to be renewed to the faith of its founders. My heritage was in this small town. My Mother's grandfather was the town carpenter and buggy maker and had helped to build this church. It was this church that my praying Great-Grandma Emma had attended. My Father's Saxon parents had settled a farm on the outskirts of town. This was where I learned to love farm life. The wonderful memories of a great childhood that this town held and being able to share my childhood home with my children was exciting to me.

The children and I began to attend church. We were accepted back as though we had never left. My heart wanted this congregation to realize that God could be as active, alive and real for them today as He was in Bible days. I wanted to tell them that He could do today what He had done in the past. Inside He said, "Walk it and you won't need to talk it." Only once did my husband ever go to church after moving back. I never pushed from that point on. He was invited and with the Lord's help I was able to leave it there when he always refused us. I had quit nagging about going to church and quit quoting Scripture to him, trying in love to walk it, not talk it, at home as well as elsewhere. The closer I walked with the Lord, the less I could be tolerated by Mike. I was learning a great lesson about the inner presence being with me.

A group of women, of which I was one, believed that the Lord would have an Aglow started in our area and as I got involved and got into the training I began to get the understanding of what the Lord had been showing me these many months. Putting God first did not mean that I attended every church service and every Bible study I could get to, and if I could not get to every prayer meeting, that was all right too.

Putting God first right now was to stay home when the Holy Spirit said to stay home and to go when He opened the way, to read my Bible in private, to minister love to my husband by taking MY pressure off and letting the Holy Spirit be the only one to put pressure on. I was determined to let the Lord show me how to walk this way, making many mistakes, but kept trying to put this new revelation of how to put God first into practice. Every move I made was wrong in Mike's eyes. The more obedient to God I became (notice I said "obedient," not "perfect") the more the scripture II Corinthians 3:18 became alive to me. It says that because we continued to behold in the Word of God as in a mirror, the glory of the Lord, we are constantly being transfigured into His very own image in ever increasing splendor and from one degree of glory to another; (for this comes from the Lord Who is the Spirit).

I was so happy in Jesus that I would just grin and shine all the time and Mike was so miserable he could not stand my joy. The Joy of Jesus truly was becoming a strength to me in the midst of trouble. This Joy remained all the time. People were always saying, "How do you do it? You smile all the time and you seem to glow?" I didn't understand it nor could I explain it. The Bible speaks about deep wells of joy and springs that bubble. He decided to let me drink of these supernatural joy waters that are there for all, whether we are at the top of the mountain or walking through a valley.

As I said, this joy was very hard for my husband to tolerate. His way of reacting was to constantly put me down. I was told

I was the worst person, worst mother, worst wife, worst cook, worst looking person to be alive. I would retreat somewhere in the house to get away from the verbal abuse. Sobbing, crying, I would sing, "the joy of the Lord is my strength," "the joy of the Lord is my strength," until I could feel that strength within me. Sometimes I sang it fifteen times and the quiet peace of the Holy Spirit would then remind me that Jesus loved me. With the confidence that Jesus loved me, I could then look back and see what truth there was in the abuse because there was correction needed, and to forgive the rest. I did not find this easy and I constantly prayed for the Lord to help me hold on. I began to realize that Mike was showing his anger toward me because I was physically there, but it was really Jesus in me that He hated. By reaching out to Jesus through prayer and this song I was kept from being consumed with self-pity.

My husband wanted us to go out on weekends with his friends to different places to eat and drink. He said this would relax him and make him happy to feel I was not so religious minded. I said, "O.K." I felt peace about this even though the question was asked, "What if Jesus came, would He stop at a bar or movie to get you?" I knew He would because I was going to those places to minister to my husband and the Lord's love is toward the sinner and the redeemed. I was raised in a non-drinking family. The taste of alcohol was not a temptation for me. I spent the time trying to be friendly, not giving any appearance of judging what anyone else did. This was not easy. Being delivered of a religious spirit, that spirit was always lurking around, hoping I would not recognize it. In my mind (soul) the battle would rage. "Why don't you just tell them how you love them and you hate to see them physically destroying their bodies this way?"

This sounds like a very good true statement, does it not? Some of it is true, but remember, the Lord told me, "Walk it." A religious spirit is very subtle. It puts enough truth in its words that if we don't test the spirits we can easily be deceived into taking back that which we have been delivered of. Jesus has given us the Holy Spirit who brings to us wonderful gifts. (I Corinthians 12) His gift of discernment can tell us which spirit we are listening to.

The Lord has been faithful to His word in I Corinthians

10:13 (Amp), "He (can be trusted) not to let you be tempted and tried and assayed beyond your ability and strength of resistance and power to endure, but with the temptation He will (always) also provide the way out — the means to escape to a landing place — that you may be capable and strong and powerful, patiently to bear up under it." If the music got too loud or they drank too much, my body would react to the smoke. Heavy smoke affected my breathing and that in turn made my crazy heart act up. Mike would take me home, knowing this was no put-on, but a real physical ailment. Coming home with tremendous burning of the lungs, coughing, wheezing and the inner battle to only react in love was very, very hard. The thoughts would come that "anyone who really cared anything about me would not ask me to sit in this atmosphere, knowing the affect it had on my health, and it is a shame you are all alone here. At least, you should be able to pray and ask Jesus to deliver you and heal your cough. It wouldn't hurt to at least call out softly the name of Jesus as a witness to those who are hurting you." Recognize it? Yes, the same religious spirit. The Lord would cut through with, "You are never alone. I have promised to never leave you or forsake you."

At times Mike would feel convicted for causing my health problems. But because I was learning to leave it with the Lord, I never had to say anything. The conviction in Mike made him react in anger toward me again for spoiling these "good times," but I was learning a lesson in unconditional love and I only felt compassion for all his misunderstanding. The tension eased for a while, especially around his friends but not around mine. His deliberate little insults and digs kept my friends away from us as a couple. The Holy Spirit was assuring me that He would never let me go too far, as long as I stayed in the Bible and walked in obedience, as best I could.

The tension grew over the next few months, but His Joy was ever more evident. I knew I was walking in Satan's territory because of pressure from Mike to give up this "religious stuff." Even though I hadn't talked about the Lord or read my Bible near him at all, and did not watch Christian T.V. while he was at home, tension was beginning to take a physical toll on me. My nerves and heart felt like tight ropes were constantly squeezing and you could sense spiritual battles taking place, even though I couldn't explain it. Never once did I feel the urge to turn my back on the Lord. His keeping power towards me was and is tremendous.

A crisis mounted in the kitchen one evening. I was very tired and walked right out of the Spirit into the flesh. As Mike verbally abused our daughter, I defended her. He then turned his abuse on me. I pushed him away very hard, and lost my temper, yelling, crying, telling him I could not take much more. He said, "Me either!" and with full rage he turned and hit my cheek and eye with his fist. I literally saw stars as I passed out. I had always wondered if that statement were true. What a way to find out! Our daughters were hysterical and thought I was dead. I woke up to being unable to see, for my eye had already swollen shut. My head felt like it had been split open. As the girls were crying and getting me ice. I heard a strong word from the Lord, "Take no offense, daughter." I was totally amazed. Those words released my anger just like air out of a balloon. I was not angry. When I told Mike I was sorry and asked forgiveness for provoking him, it almost did him in. Finally, I got a look at my face; I felt sick. My head hurt so badly! I knew I had a concussion. I hurt so badly inside and outside that I thought if I died it would be a blessing. The doctor was sure that my cheekbone was fractured; all the signs were there. All I could say was, "Oh, Lord, please, not that!" He didn't fail me because the doctor was very surprised when he came back with the X-ray — no fracture. Something died that day, not compassion or love for Mike, but my hope that he loved me even in a small way. That realization was very hard to deal with. It was like death had occurred in the family. Oh, Lord help me! He brought to my remembrance the vision of His mountain and I dusted it off and took it off the shelf as He directed me to in Scripture: Exodus 33:14. He said, "My presence shall go with you (v. 21). Then the Lord said, "Behold, there is a place by Me, and you shall stand there on the rock; (v. 22) "and it will come about, while My glory is passing by, that I will put you in the cleft of the rock and cover you with My hand until I have passed by." WOW! An instantaneous shot of His divine caring for me flooded over my soul. I didn't know that was in the Scripture. I thought it was just in the movie. His caring for all of us is beyond my comprehension. When I found the next one, (Psalm 20), "Thou shalt hide (hide by covering) them in the secret (secret place) of thy presence," I

rejoiced. How I needed to be hidden from the hurt.
Your testimony:

> Has a sudden move or situation ever moved you from a place of comfort? How did you feel? How did you know God was in it? What new spiritual blessing opened up to you?
>
> Has the Lord ever called you to "walk it, not talk it"?
>
> Has your family ever had trouble with the Holy Spirit in you?
>
> Have you ever had to be in the world — but not of it?
>
> Have you ever felt something die between you and someone else? What died? How did you feel?

## About the chart . . .

**A Couple of Examples:**
>  1) **Work — Home**
>
>  If husband insists wife stay home from job and help cut wood and employer sees her and she gets fired, she cannot say that her husband made her do it. Her responsibility was to be a good worker. Work and home overlapped.
>
>  2) **Church — Home**
>
>  Minister appealing for funds, strongly, to brother in church and husband goes home and says that the family will do without milk this week. Church overruling the husband in the area of protecting and caring for his family.
>
>  3) Let's take a tough one. A woman is called of God to the role of evangelist or even pastor. In the area of ministry, the church leader is over her. In the home the husband is still over her, and if he will not recognize her call, the husband is in trouble with God. He is overlapping roles.

**GOD**

Four realms of designated authority in the kingdom. He says to obey them.

None of these conflict when you are under the right head.

Acts 5:29 — Peter and other apostles replied, "We must obey God rather than men."

**HOME**
Husband — responsible to protect and guard.

**CHURCH**
Prophet — pastor — apostle only in realm of ministry.

**WORK**
Master — Employer

**CIVIL**
Judges — Kings — President
Police

---

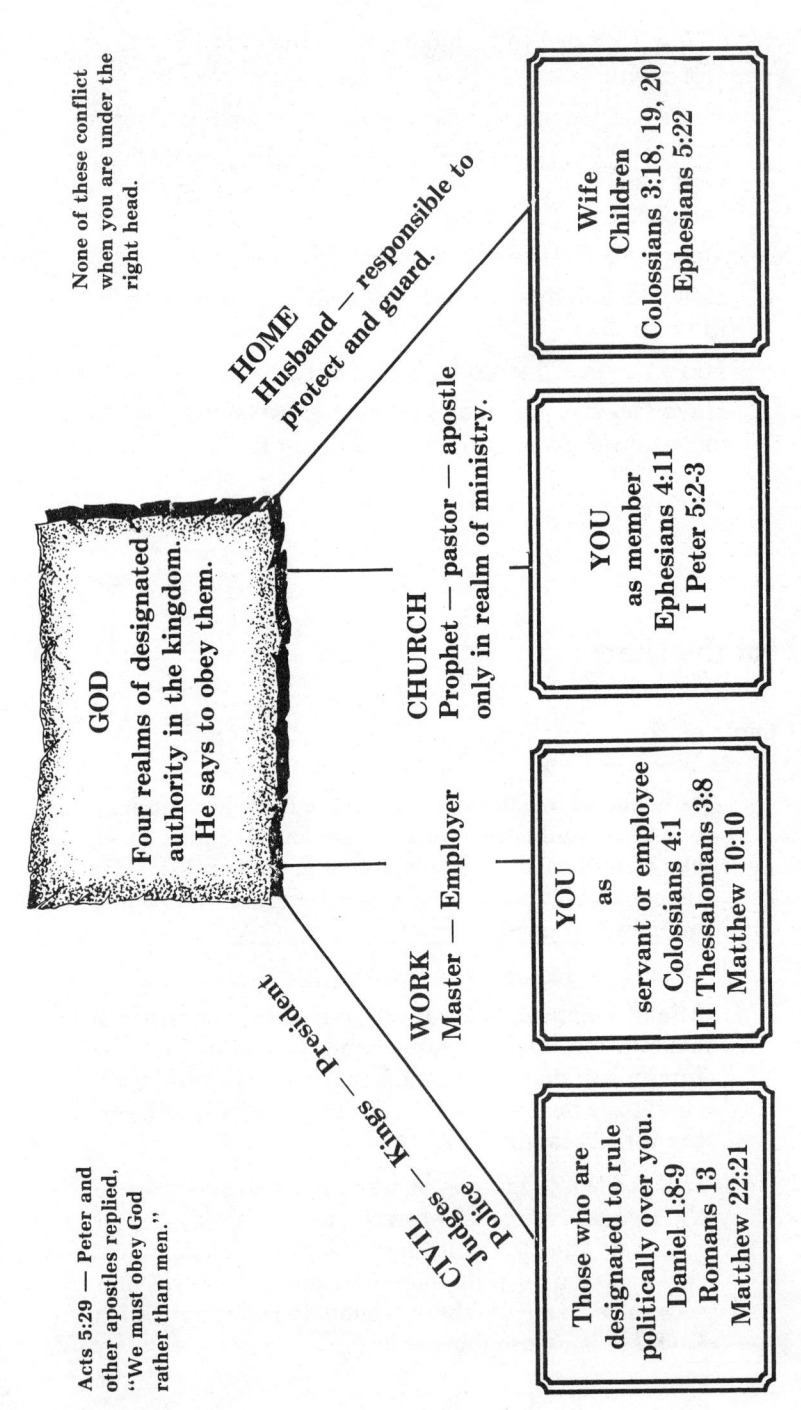

Wife
Children
Colossians 3:18, 19, 20
Ephesians 5:22

YOU
as member
Ephesians 4:11
I Peter 5:2-3

YOU
as
servant or employee
Colossians 4:1
II Thessalonians 3:8
Matthew 10:10

Those who are designated to rule politically over you.
Daniel 1:8-9
Romans 13
Matthew 22:21

**GOVERNMENT OF GOD**

Peg, Laurie, Carla in our pool

Lee, Laurie, Peggy cutting grass back of pool

Linda across from Golden Gate

Linda in Israel — made it!

**Worth it all. Laurie, Lee, Peg.**

**Mario, Timothy, Megan, Mellissa, Grandma, Marcella**

My ordination at Gloryland

Linda & Ben — 700 Club

# XVIII
# I Can't Take Anymore!

My Aglow meeting was in a few days. It was a meeting where husbands were invited and I was the president. "What am I going to say, Lord? I'll have to wear sunglasses."

He said, "Linda, I am going to ask you to protect Mike for me. You are to build him up even in this, for if you have forgiven, it is forgotten. Right?" Then the most amazing thing happened. Mike said he would go to the meeting with me. As Mike listened to our speakers, Russ and Norma Bixler, Russ said he had to come to the place where he released his wife to be what the Lord had called her to be. It was a good meeting. I prayed that Mike heard some of what was said.

When anyone asked what had happened to me, I calmly told them that I had fallen and struck my cheek on the edge of our step. It was partly true. After the meeting, my ears could hardly believe it when Mike said, "The Lord told me that I could hold you no longer from His call on your life."

I felt as though I were in sock. My first thought was, "What makes you think YOU can hear God?" Uh, oh, there it tried to go again. I knew what was wrong. But within a week something seemed to break in Mike. He totally released his fury toward me. He cursed me in the name of Satan. In my presence, he prayed that my heart would quit and he told me that every day he prayed to Satan to kill me. I felt that at first these statements were to shock me and to make fun of me. I begged him not to play around with those kind of prayers, but the more I acknowledged the prayers, the worse it got.

I cried to God, "I don't know how much more I can take!" He would respond, "My word says I'll never give more than you can take. Right?" Mike was becoming deeply depressed. I thank God for the gift of discernment. We were in a spiritual battle. I needed to discern between Mike and Satan to see which one was cursing me, who was in control at which time.

I prayed for Mike, realizing that he was not the enemy. One day Laurie said, "Mom, sometimes I see Dad in his eyes, but when he starts yelling, I can see him change. It is really scaring me." In his heart my companion wanted me dead. The only way out for him was for me to die, for I had repeatedly told him that I could not walk away from the marriage and feel I was being right with the Lord. Some of my physical problems were the result of Mike's prayers to Satan, asking him to have control, to cause my heart to stop. But because the Lord Jesus was God of my life, Satan could only exert pressure and try to get me to believe his lies. I read and reread Romans 8:6-18 NAS.

My last heart examination had been such a good one. When I went this time the doctor said, "What has happened? Your blood pressure is terrible. Your heart arrhythmia is very bad. Linda, whatever you are doing, quit it. Tension is killing you." I cried and cried all the way home from his office. I talked to the Lord. "I've made a covenant, Lord, to remain with Mike until death." It hit me! "Lord, do you require of me to lay down my life for someone who hates me?"

Who says Satan is his god? My first reaction was, "NO, sir, I am not going to do it; what would the children do?" I felt a dramatic silence in me. I did not understand it. I remembered when I had made a vow many years before, after God had healed me of epilepsy and because I was so thankful and amazed that He would do this for ME. I told the Lord I was setting my heart to find Him. He had come so far to reach me and heal me that I would set my heart toward Him even if I died along the way. Driving along — crying, struggling, having to keep the car on the road and thinking that had I known these would be the circumstances of which the Lord would remind me, I would probably never have said that; yet, I did vow, and so it had to be. "Lord, if I die, I'll die," saying that with my lips only. I was struggling to mean it.

I did not know that I had set God's Word in motion by my vow. David had said that he had set the Lord continually before him: "because He is at my right hand, I shall not be moved. Therefore my heart is glad and my glory (my inner self) rejoices; my body too shall rest and confidently dwell in safety. for You will not abandon me to Sheol (the place of the dead), neither will You suffer Your holy one to see corruption. You will show me the path of life; *in Your presence is fullness of joy, at Your right hand there are pleasures for evermore.*" (Psalm 16:6-11 AMP.)

I was being devastated by name calling — hurt — ungodly prayers and yet in my spirit I wasn't. "Who among you fears the Lord and obeys the word of his servant? Let him who walks in the dark, who has no light trust in the name of the Lord and rely on his God." (Isaiah 50:10) The Holy Spirit was with me, helping me to rely on God even in this terrible darkness, so I can say with confidence, "The Lord is my helper. I will not be afraid. What can man do to me?" (Hebrews 13:6 NIV)

Paul said one of the reasons he was suffering, yet he was not ashamed was because he knew whom he believed in and was convinced that He is able to guard what he had entrusted to Him for that day. (II Timothy 1:12 NIV) And supernaturally, because of the Holy Spirit that was being stirred within me and because I knew He had guarded great grandma's prayers, He would guard mine also. The Spirit was comforting, encouraging, doing all that He says He will do, and yet the enemy was constantly at my mind, with fear of leaving the children — doubt — what a battle for my mind, but Praise be to God — greater is He that is within me than he that is in the world. The Holy Spirit won as I finally could say that dying only meant that I would get to go to the place of peace that I had once experienced with the Lord. If my dying would help Mike, then my work would be finished, and I would go. What does it matter what we go through, people, as long as we have the presence of the Lord with us. I was committed to the intent of the Lord.

My Lord did even more in me with that commitment. This wonderful joy that He gives was even more evident. Even people who knew us could not tell how bad it was because of the Joy of the Lord that ran through me that covered the desperate situation. My husband did not look at me. He seemed to be always talking to me with his back turned. I felt so sorry. I knew he was struggling with the Holy Spirit and with the spirit from hell. He would not let me say anything to him of a ministry nature. I saw his depression get worse and worse. This made his anger turn on all of us with the thoughts of destroying either himself or me. Is that not like Satan? If he can't get one, then he will try to destroy the other? But we were praying, and Satan could not take either life.

Suddenly, one day my husband packed his things and said

"Goodbye." I was stunned. "Lord, what is happening? What about all this love, obedience? I thought it was to be a glorious restoration. He is supposed to get saved!!" I ran to the basement, sat in a corner by the pool in the dark. "I'm going to be hysterical." But I couldn't. "Well, I'm going to cry my eyes out." But I couldn't. "There's something wrong here. I need to be hysterical. My husband just left." Before I got too carried away, God's words came quietly and firmly. "If the unbeliever depart, let him depart." Right away I answered back, "I don't believe that is scriptural." So I looked it up. (I Corinthians 7:15 NAS) It really does say that if the unbelieving one leaves to let him leave.

In my mind I now had this great dramatic reconciliation. After he was out from under the blessing of a Christian wife, etc., etc., etc., he would be back, etc., etc. I would turn one day in church and see him racing down the aisle to the Lord and me. I was stretching it a bit. In fact, after a few weeks of kicking up his heels, he decided that maybe we could live in the same house, but go our separate ways. Of course, I would need to get some counseling and get rid of all this religious stuff and he would live in the back of the house and go as he pleased, but that way we would not lose all the material things we had accumulated. I listened for direction. The Lord's quiet words to me were, "Return not to Egypt." You will hear with your spiritual ear if there has been a heart change.

I questioned the Lord. Why this after all these years? Why could I not have divorced him for adultery in the beginning — before these long years had passed? Finally He answered me, "That is forgivable and forgettable." Well, then, Lord, why after all this physical and mental abuse, was I not permitted to leave before I had to endure all this? He again answered, "I endured much more for you. I will never let you be stretched beyond what I know you are capable of bearing. Trust me. Everything before has all been forgivable, daughter."

Then why now, Lord? I heard His answer. "The covenant was finally broken."

I did not understand, so I had to do some digging in the Word and seeking about what the Lord was saying. I discovered that in my situation any and all previous offenses were forgivable because the Lord had forgiven all such sins Himself in many parts of the Bible. I still had been reaping what I had sown in rebellion, but now the harvest was ready.

There is a covenant of companionship that is made when you

decide to get married, long before the official vows. It is made before the sexual part of marriage. I has to do with agreeing to take care of, love, be a friend, be a companion. (*Marriage — Divorce and Remarriage* by J. Adams) The Lord said to me, "That has been broken. This is the only reason I am permitting this to go this direction." This was not an unforgivable sin. It was just that Mike's heart had hardened and God would not allow murder or suicide.

Mike still had the choice of his will. I prayed for him almost totally in my spiritual prayer language so that my emotions would not get in the way of my prayers being right as it says in Romans 8:26-27 (NAS). "And in the same way the Spirit also helps our weakness; for we do not know how to pray as we should, but the Spirit Himself intercedes for us with groanings too deep for words."

Mike chose to divorce. I agreed to a dissolutionment. He remarried shortly afterward. Psalm 68:19 says, "Blessed be the Lord, who bears our burdens and carries us day by day, even the God who is our salvation! Selah. The Lord seemed to wrap my emotions in a bubble. I thought I should be hysterical. I had no job and have not worked for years. When I should have been crying, I found that I had overwhelming peace.

It was not all easy. Nor did I adjust in one day. Sometimes the thoughts came, "Well, *if* I had done it this way . . ." The Lord would gently say, "Have you asked for my forgiveness?" "Yes, Lord." "Then, Linda, you are trying to pick up your burdens again."

I would try to lay my burdens down again. As the Lord let my emotions slowly out of the bubble, He helped me to handle them. When self pity came, I would be saying, "Well, he never loved me, Boo Hoo!" The Lord would say, "But I have loved you. Remember his childhood. He just doesn't know how. Forgive him." "But, Lord, he promised to go to church with me from the beginning." "Yes, Linda, but did I not try to warn you in the beginning?" "Yes, Lord, I'm sorry."

Somehow the Lord God of Mercy kept me in this running conversation of forgiveness for a long time, helping me to see my part and Mike's part. This kept me walking in an attitude of forgiveness which was above my humaness. This constant forgiving of the Lord to me helped me when I came to the part of the Bible where it says, "God hates divorce." I could say that I hate it, too! God hates what it does to the children, to the parents, to the in-laws, to the friends, to me, what a large circle of hurt it causes. I knew, though, that God did not hate me. He had proven His love and caring for me and no one could cause me to feel condemned. I had walked with His Spirit through this, not perfectly, but with determination to do it God's way, and I was forgiven. I knew His forgiveness and I was free.

I knew I could not put the children in the middle and tried to help them to forgive us both. I haven't reached perfection in this either, but I am working on it.

I got busy where I could give out and not sit back in pity. I became a 700 Club phone counselor, worked in Aglow, watched Christian T.V. The Lord began to speak to me through the body of Christ.

A sister in Aglow who lived in southern Ohio, a minister in a prayer meeting, a caller on the phones at 700 Club — each separately gave me the Scripture, I Corinthians 16:9. The Lord was opening a door to me. I was getting exciting about this door that was to open. What happened was that I had to sell my home because I could not keep up the monthly payments. I could hardly face this. It was like selling half of my heart. It was my family home. Half of my childhood had been spent here and many years of my children's lives were spent there.

Finally, when I was ready to listen, the Lord seemed to say, "Is this the kind of treasure that you can lay up in heaven?" "Oh, Lord, I'm doing it again. Forgive me! This is only brick and wood and I willingly lay this at your feet. But you are going to have to help me." He reassured me that the treasures of this home were in my heart and would never be removed but that I was holding on to an earthly possession.

Still, I said, "Lord, are you sure all this is not just me? Could you please give me a sign? After all I have lost, are you sure you want me to lose the house, too?" I went about my business, keeping the house up, putting it up for sale. One day I was riding the lawn mower, cutting my beautiful three acres of grass and riding in the woods to the back. Looking toward the enclosed swimming pool that had meant so much to my Dad and me, I gave thanks for the beautiful place in which I had been raised. I thanked Him for the beautiful trees that were there. I suddenly remembered an old rose bush that had not bloomed for seven or so years. I thought I would check on taking out the old bush. As I drove around a big lilac bush, "WOW! There was the old rose bush covered with roses! It was in the darkest red filled with blooms. I began to cry. It was my sign. I knew it. I raced to the phone to call Mom to ask how many years it had been since she could remember it blooming. More than seven, she thought. Truly, when you praise Him and are thankful in the midst of your circumstances, He does wonders!

Your testimony:

> Have you ever been aware of curses or negative prayers affecting your life? Have you ever prayed against someone?
>
> Have you ever physically felt the effects of spiritual warfare in your life? How did you cope?
>
> Has a situation or relationship ever changed totally from what you thought God would do or allow?
>
> What worldly treasures have you had to let go of?
>
> Have you ever asked God for a sign?

# XIX
# A Dress Of Gold

Then a door did open. One I could never have thought possible for a small-town gal in Ohio. The 700 Club was coming to my house with television cameras to film testimony of my epilepsy healing. They wanted to film my house, my children, my church, my town, my school, my friends, my parents. How could I be more blessed than to have this forever on tape and shown to millions of people as a witness of the healing power of Christ!

I have experienced healing by calling on the Name of Jesus. He has saved my life from death by His mercy and faithfulness and using nurses and doctors. My arthritis was healed by hearing His Word preached. My arthritic symptoms were overcome by rebuking Satan in His name. Others have prayed and fasted for me and there have been parts that were not healed the way I thought. I am still believing for my heart to be completely healed. There have been many difficult days with my heart, times when it became so good that it was working close to perfect, then there have been times that have been inexplicable.

The Bible says "Not by might nor by power, but by my spirit says the Lord." (Zechariah 4:6) The Lord by His Spirit is always (or should be) changing us — changing us into the likeness of Jesus.

Grace is a mighty word — it is the word of God's character and produces Holiness. It is the word the Holy Spirit is speaking to His church in this time.

Since we are constantly being changed, as I was driving to a meeting in August with Winnie, one of my God given sisters, she was praying for the meeting and she stopped and said, "Ohhhh, I see God dressing you in a golden dress. It is gossamer gold and the sleeves are layered, looking something like feathers. It is long and flowing, but it is gossamer. God is dressing you in His love."

WOW! O.K., I can handle a golden dress. I don't understand all that, but it sounded great. I wrote it down so I would not forget what was said and looked up the word gossamer — fine web like threads — can be seen through. I knew that meant to be transparent, to be real, not super spiritual or prideful. I thought, "Hmmmmmm, gold — well, maybe glory — love all sounds great."

About two weeks later I became ill. I began to cough and cough and wheeze. Then I had a fever. I could not work. I became so weak, so short of breath. The doctor said it was pneumonia — then the old bronchial asthma began kicking up. You see, I have had so many medications in my life, I am allergic to all antibiotics and all heart medications. Lungs are beginning to fill from congestive heart failure, speaking the Word, rebuking Satan, claiming my inheritance. Every prayer chain that I knew of was praying. My lungs were tightening. I cannot be put in the hospital because when my husband left, my insurance companies all cancelled, and no one else would insure me. The doctors were perplexed and in the midst of this, I had many months earlier been given a gift of a trip to Israel in November for my birthday — my heart's one desire. It was too close to the date to cancel and get my money back.

The WORD from some of the ladies who were praying was REST. Rest. I said I didn't know how to rest because I knew I was dying and I couldn't lie down to rest my body because my lungs were full. The word I kept hearing was STAND.

I was getting angry at Satan and was binding him and casting him out. Everything I knew to do in the Lord, I was doing, and it still seemed as though I would miss taking my trip.

I asked my heart doctor if I could try Cortizone. That had helped one other time when I had had this coughing and congestive heart failure. So we did, and two days later I left for Israel. I was able to persevere and go. I still wasn't well, but felt almost back to normal.

I landed finally in the land where He had physically walked. I cried for the first two days and was careful to measure how much I walked, and I got to go almost everywhere the tour walked. My dream, my prayer, was happening. It was great. The cortizone was finished the day before we were to fly home. That night everything returned, the cough, fever, filling of my lungs, my heart running wild. I knew that the airline would not let me fly in this condition. I was with a tour from my Bible school and we prayed. It did not move, so I borrowed two cortizone pills from one of the ladies who had arthritis, and I made it home, as sick as I was before I left. The energy to talk with all the gurgling and wheezing was too much. My friends would call and ask how I was doing and all I could do was wheeze. They would tell me not to talk, that we would just pray. It stayed. I was so tired, and I just kept asking the Lord why He didn't just take me home. All I perceived was stand, Stand, STAND.

Doubt kept a constant battle, after all God was supposed to have done for me, was it my own power that had helped me, not God! The accuser was around with his army of demons.

But He who has begun a good work in me will perfect it — I stand, I believe in His goodness. I believe . . .

I was flipping through the Bible, saying, "Lord," and I stopped at I Peter 1:6-8. I surely was in the fire. I felt fire in my lungs. My faith was certainly being tried in fire, and I hoped it was more than perishable gold. No one had an answer — if I had enough faith — I didn't have any faith when He healed me of epilepsy, but my faith had grown, but inside I felt a check. I did have the Word and I was standing. It was not moving, but I knew I had to be careful of unbalance. I took my authority as His daughter. It seemed to take its authority and look right back at me. "How, Lord, can Satan have this much control when I belong to You? How!!"

I cried daily, "Lord, have mercy, give me understanding. I know and believe in your goodness. I know you have good in mind for me. You have proven that." On one of the days when I was again repeating this, He seemed to say quietly, "What if I did choose this?" I immediately rebuked that. I heard no further word from Him until I said, "Lord, was that You? I do not want to be disrespectful, but that is not what most say!" The small voice said for me to read Job 1. "Now, Lord, I know what Job says. That is Old Testament." I read it and turned on to Job 2:3-6, and I personalized it.

Then the Lord said to Satan, "Have you considered my servant Linda? There is no one on earth like her; she is blameless and upright, (Because of Jesus) a woman who fears God and shuns evil. And she still maintains her integrity, though you incited me against her to ruin her without any reason."

"Skin for skin!" Satan replied. "A woman will all she has for her own life. But stretch out your hand and strike her flesh and bones, and she will surely curse you to your face."

The Lord said to Satan, "Very well, then, she is in your hands; but you must spare her life."

"Oh, Lord, you do have control of this and at that revelation, I daily began to get well. For the first time since last August, I remembered my golden dress. It was taking much fire to weave the thread.

God did not bring the sickness. He created the world without sickness. Satan saw that sickness arrived and Satan brought the sickness to me and thought he would do me in . . . but God said, "No, you can try her, but not kill her and because I am sovereign God to her, I will change what you meant for evil into a dress of gold that will help her change and become enlarged in spirit and holiness." Jesus left for us a tremendous asset. His name is Holy Spirit, He has for us gifts that are for the benefit of His people. The gift of discernment is one we need to desire, to enable us to recognize good and evil. Is it any wonder Satan likes to keep these gifts out of the denominations?

The Lord takes the experiences of your life or the seasons of your life to make us into the likeness of His perfect servant Jesus, but He will also take those experiences out of our lives if we pout, stomp our feet, cry out all His words back at Him. He will lift the season, but we will be left without the complete work done in us. The Lord just says, "O.K., have your way and instead of change, just go one more time around the mountain."

I thank Him that He helped me through this one that I did not have to take one more trip around. The more I see the seasons, the more I can rejoice in the testing, for my God is the Lord of my life and that makes Satan get so small. I also know that as I pass the test of changing, I am heading for new wonders in God.

God calls us with the purpose He has for us in mind. He knows what we are capable of and what He dreams for us. That is why He never gives you more than you can take. No, He is not standing with a big stick, saying that they failed, but we'll get them, but He knows what we need. To be changed. He has tested by experiences all through the Bible. Adam and Eve, Noah, Moses, Abraham, Jesus, Paul. Why does He test? He waits to see what our response will be — positive or negative.

Why? So He can bring us on to the perfect covenant with Him.

And now as I begin to dust off the second part of the vision from quite a few years ago I realize Jesus is my high priest and that He had stopped on the steps and invited me, ME, to come up into a place of knowing Him so well that He and I might talk and fellowship together to make His heart glad.

The Bible describes my vision so well in Psalms 27:4-5 NAS. One thing have I desired of the Lord, that I will seek after; that I may dwell in the house of the Lord all the days of my life, to behold the beauty of the Lord, and to enquire in his temple. For in the time of trouble, he shall hide me in his pavilion; in the secret of his tabernacle shall he hide me; He will lift me up on a rock.

He worked so many years on getting me in physical shape and then it took so long for me to let my mind be renewed but He never quit, nor did He get tired of me. Just as with you, He says to come up so that we may know Him. Will you take one moment and enquire of the Lord? He has an answer for you, too! You are as individual to Him as I am.

And as Paul . . . I have every confidence, with my whole being, that He who began a good work in us will perfect it until the day of Jesus Christ. What blessing! What joy! What love!

Blessings upon you,
Linda

## A final word . . .

Many doors have opened for me to share that portion of Christ I know so personally. I have shared at numerous Women's Aglow meetings, at churches, Christian television programs, singles' retreats. I have been studying to show myself approved. I have a Bible teacher's certificate from International Bible Institute and Seminary, Orlando, Florida, was ordained at Gloryland Fellowship of Churches and Ministers International, Florence, S. C. I am a former Operation Blessing Coordinator, CBN, Youngstown, Ohio and also a 700 Club Counselor. I teach a Bible class at my church and am also a layleader. I work with the United Methodist Renewal Service Fellowship, Nashville, Tennessee. I have been an Area Board officer for Women Aglow.

Yet, I am so aware that there is so much more He wants to show me of Himself.

*In loving memory and great thanksgiving for Lee Michael Gregorino.*

*As we got ready for this second printing my beloved son went home to be with Jesus after a tragic accident. He was his mother's protector and encourager from his youth. Jesus had made him one of the best young husbands and fathers I ever saw (Psalms 42:3).*

*My tears have been my food day and night while men say to me all day long, "Where is your God?"*

*"Why? Why?" is my cry, but yet I hear "Can you trust and will you persevere?"*

*Dresses of gold are not easy to come by!*

*Linda Gregorino*

## *In 6 Days*

### *by C.H. McGowen, M.D.*

A book that has served to explain
the active creation to over 50,000 readers.

FROM SON-RISE

### $3.95

---

*For a complete listing of our seminars, books and tapes, contact:*

James W. Biros • Florence Biros

412-946-8334

**SON-RISE**
**Publications & Distribution Co.**

Rte. 3, P.O. Box 202
New Wilmington, PA 16142

*"We aim to have HIS SON-rise in every heart."*